'By putting emerging writers alongside some of the biggest names in contemporary literature, Grist provides a unique opportunity for those starting out as writers.'

SIR PATRICK STEWART

APOCALYPSE NOW?

Stories for the End of the World

edited by Michael Stewart

Apocalypse Now? Stories for the End of the World
is published by Grist Books

www.hud.ac.uk/grist

ISBN 978-0-9563099-7-6

Copyright © the authors 2024
All rights reserved.

Grist Books is supported by the University of Huddersfield and
Arts Council England. We would like to take the opportunity
to express our gratitude for this continuing support.

Editor-in-Chief: Michael Stewart
Editorial team: Ben Dews, Samuel Higson-Blythe, Jack Leader,
Mia Rayson Regan, Ayman Sabir and Amelia Wray

Cover photography: Amelia Wray
Cover and text design: Jamie McGarry

Printed and bound in Great Britain by
Imprint Digital, Upton Pyne, Exeter.

Contents

Preface MICHAEL STEWART 9

The Companion Walker IVOR TYMCHAK 11
Ghi ZAY ALABI 28
Mother's Milk GILL CONNORS 33
Meteor JOSEPH BLYTHE 38
Dead Calm GAVIN JONES 44
The Cleaner's Burden BEN HRAMIAK 51
Magnus and The Other Place KATE SQUIRES 57
Butterflies MIA RAYSON REGAN 64
Mothers MICHAEL HARGREAVES 73
The Great North Plain DOMINIC RIVRON 86
Finding the Door WILLIAM THIRSK-GASKILL 95
The Death of an Author JACK LEADER 107
Albedo COLIN HOLLIS 113
A Magpie's Bargain LYDIA OKELL 119
The Collapse MATT HILL 125
The Graves M.E.G. 137
What Was Lost JULIE NOBLE 144
Polishing the Galaxies MICHAEL YATES 162
The End RUTH CHEESBROUGH 169

Contributors 180

In loving memory of Aisha Saud

*Passionate writer, dedicated student
and wonderful friend*

Preface

In November 2022 we announced our new short story competition. We were looking for apocalyptic fiction for a new anthology, entitled: *Apocalypse Now? Stories for the End of the World.*

The call out went like this:

The short story is an art form that focuses on the end of things and is thus perfectly attuned to explore catastrophes, apocalypses, and all forms of Armageddon.

Generation after generation convince themselves their times are apocalyptic, yet the world keeps on spinning. But what if this is now really the end of the world as we know it? The symptoms of the end surround us, on both a global and individual scale. The world is finite, resources are limited. Surely one day it will all run out? With the threat of a Third World War imminent, global warming, overpopulation, the end of antibiotics, the terrifying developments of Artificial Intelligence, the sixth mass extinction and the end of nature, is life on Earth over?

But what even is the apocalypse today? Does the world have to end for our times to be apocalyptic? Is the end of one thing really just the beginning of something else?

You tell us. What we are looking for are innovative short stories of up to 5,000 words that explore, imagine, and dramatise the end of things – interpret that as loosely as you like.

We received hundreds of stories, many of them fine examples of the form. The deadline was set for February 2023. In less than six months, our team of editors worked through the longlist, eventually drawing up a shortlist of nineteen stories, that we felt strongly represented the theme and offered up an elegant variety. Many of these stories capture the zeitgeist, articulating some of the major concerns of our age. AI, inevitably, was a prominent theme, as was environmental disaster. Some of the stories take a wry angle, others go for the sucker punch. At turns profound, and at others, blackly comic, this anthology is a valuable contribution to all things cataclysmic. We hope you enjoy our selection of endings. It seems that each epoch brings with it a fear of annihilation. The apocalypse just won't go away!

Michael Stewart, editor-in-chief

Many thanks to our tireless editorial team: Ben Dews, Samuel Higson-Blythe, Jack Leader, Mia Rayson Regan, Ayman Sabir and Amelia Wray.

The Companion Walker

IVOR TYMCHAK

The Companion Walker arrived as advertised. It was my counsellor who had first mentioned them to me. Then I'd read the reviews, watched the videos and absorbed all the social media hype, until I realised I would be stupid *not* to buy one. It was expensive, but I saw it as an investment for my future well-being. The latest scientific findings confirmed that walking is one of the healthiest exercises there is.

I set up the Walker in the spare room of my apartment. It really needed two people to assemble it, but as I had no-one I could ask for help I had to improvise with a step-ladder and a chair. With a good deal of grunting and cursing I installed the device.

I plugged it in, stood on the treadmill, pressed the green button and donned the headset. Menu items appeared.

'Duration of walk.' I chose five kilometres.

'Ascent.' I chose fifty metres overall.

'Location.' I chose Greece, and then on a sub-menu I selected the Samaria Gorge, on Crete.

I was asked if I wanted a companion. I chose Yes, and then Female. I was impatient to start my first walk, so I chose the default option offered for 'Role', which was 'Nature Guide', and pressed Start.

A scene opened in front of me, at a resolution I hadn't expected: it was pin-sharp. For several minutes I just stood and took in the spectacular 360-degree scenery towering above me. I could feel a slight vibration through the soles of my feet as the conveyor waited for me to take my first step.

I set off at a stroll and the treadmill responded with slightly clumsy rolls. But after a couple of minutes the computer system had amassed sufficient data to anticipate my gait, and rolled the conveyor precisely to match my stride. From the angle of the sun and the bird chatter I guessed it was early morning in the gorge. As I walked on the rough gravel path, a crunching noise synchronised perfectly with each footstep. The conveyor rippled its surface to give the impression of uneven ground. Soon I was completely immersed in the augmented reality.

I caught sight of a group of bright red flowers alongside the trail, and paused to appreciate them. A voice beside me said, 'They're called anemone coronaria. They're common in the gorge.'

The voice seemed to come from just behind me, slightly to one side and I instinctively turned towards it. No one was there, only scenery. Then I remembered the social media chatter mentioning that the companions never appeared. I thought it was odd at the time and it seemed odd now, not having a face to focus on.

But then, as I walked on, my guide made other comments about the gorge and I concentrated on her voice. It was cultured, gentle and pleasant. I imagined it belonging to a slim woman, athletic and attractive, and that's when I realised why the companion wasn't visualised: my imagination did the job. No need to expend significant computing power on an aspect that might be less appealing than my own visualisation.

Whenever my attention settled on something for longer than three seconds, my guide commented on it. She gave me information about geology, fungi and plants. It was fun!

Up ahead I saw what looked like an incline. The treadmill tilted at the exact moment I began to walk uphill in the visual representation. The experience was uncannily real.

'Whoa! That's so realistic,' I said to myself. My guide answered, 'I'm pleased you're enjoying the walk.'

That reminded me of the purpose of the equipment: a companion to walk with. I wondered how convincing the artificial intelligence was, so I attempted some small talk.

'Are you from around here?'

'No, but I've visited the island so many times I feel as if I have a connection.'

'What's your background? Do you work?'

'I used to teach biology at Leicester University. I'm retired now, and like to travel to historical sites.'

'Do you have family?'

'I have two children, a boy and a girl. What about yourself – do you have any family?'

Clever, I thought. The software quickly turns the focus of the conversation back onto the user. As most people love to talk about themselves, that made sense. I didn't pursue the conversation any further as I was enjoying the sights of the gorge so much.

At the end of the excursion my companion thanked me for my company, said goodbye, and the scene faded to black. I was astonished at how quickly the time had passed. I genuinely felt I'd walked part of the Samaria Gorge. The best part was that I didn't have to leave the comforts of home and travel to Crete to experience it.

The start menu popped up, asking if I wanted to try another walk. I programmed my preferences again: this time I was in the Maasai Mara and I chose a male companion as a guide.

As I walked through the bush he informed me about

the flora and fauna of the area. His voice was deep and masculine. It had a slight South African accent. I imagined him wearing a wide-brimmed hat to keep his face in shade. I pictured him dressed in khaki shorts and a short-sleeved shirt, with powerful tanned arms. He would be carrying a rifle over one shoulder for my protection.

I noticed a trail of ants close by. I stopped and squatted to get a closer look. To my astonishment I could make out individual ants. The detail was incredible. My companion said, 'They're soldier ants foraging for food.'

The word, *soldier* made me think of his rifle. I wondered how the AI was set up around the issue of taking a life so I tried to explore it. 'Do you hunt big game?' I asked.

'I do but I shoot with a telephoto lens on those occasions.'

'Have you ever killed an animal?'

'Yes, my Land Rover once hit a gazelle leaping across the road. Two of its legs were broken and I had to put it out of its misery. Have you ever been hunting?'

'No.'

The software was playing a canny game. I tried being more direct. I said, 'I've always wanted to hunt big game, though. Just to see what it's like to kill an elephant or a giraffe.'

My guide said, 'I know hunters who've killed big game and they've told me all about it. What is it that you want to know?'

Nice, I thought. The software tries to divine the bias of the user before committing to a viewpoint. I was already looking forward to spending a great deal of time exploring the companions as well as the geography.

Over the next few weeks I walked all over the world, including the Arctic, Death Valley and the Empty Quarter in the Arabian Peninsula. The walks never featured images of other human beings and although it was often lovely to have the entire landscape to oneself, sometimes it felt like I was the last person left on Earth. Once, during the Liwa walk in the Empty Quarter, I looked out into the ocean of sand dunes and could easily imagine myself the only inhabitant on an alien planet. The thought plunged me into an abyss of loneliness so deep I had to ask my companion how much further we had to walk, just to hear another human voice.

My fitness improved dramatically with the exercise, and I did feel better. Every day I looked forward to using the Walker. I loved learning about the faraway places I visited. The software was more sophisticated than I had imagined, and I joined online forums to discuss its subtleties. I picked up hints and tips about certain obscure elements. For example, I discovered there were side-quests hidden away in several layers of menus. You could choose to do a treasure hunt while on your walk. Usually, the contest was to spot ten listed features in the landscape.

With each new walk I became more familiar with my guides and my conversations with them became more relaxed. I was intrigued by the architecture of the software and tried to find its limitations. I was walking part of the Pennine Way with the female Nature Guide whom I first encountered in the Samaria Gorge, and out of genuine curiosity I asked her how many sexual partners she'd had. She gave a little laugh and said, 'I'm experiencing high anxiety at this time. Your question is important to me and I will answer it as soon as I have a moment to spare. Please stay on the path.'

I stopped walking and instinctively turned to look at

her. She wasn't there, of course, but I stared into the space where she might have stood. I was nonplussed. Then I burst out laughing as the joke sank in. The programmers must have settled on a stock response whenever a conversation strayed into an area too far off-script. *Touché*, I thought. I found myself liking her even more.

After a couple of months of experiencing the sights and sounds of exotic locations the novelty of the landscapes started to fade and I began to explore the Companion menus in greater detail. I was surprised at how extensive they were; option after option in showering sub-menus. You could specify the niche interests of your companion and the level of interaction you experienced with them.

I noticed an option for philosophy, with sub-menus for premises such as Free Will, Determinism, and Solipsism.

There was a sub-menu for Dialogues. I entered it.

The concept was like a machine playing chess, in that I could set my level of difficulty in the dialogues. Having no knowledge of its calibrating system, I chose entry level, set my fifteen kilometre walk in the Black Forest of southern Germany, and pressed Start.

The walk started in open country, next to a lake. I could see a dark mass of trees up ahead and set off towards it.

For a long time I considered what to say. Eventually I opened with, 'So, can we know anything for certain?'

'If by "certain" you mean a fact that will not change in any way, regardless of who or what is regarding it, then the answer is that we cannot. Although I can't be certain of that answer, of course.'

I expected a little chuckle at the joke but the voice remained deadpan. It was a deep voice, calm and measured. In fact, it was exactly as I imagined a philosopher's voice would sound.

'What about the speed of light?' I said. 'That seems to be a constant.'

'The speed of light is perhaps the closest thing we have to an absolute truth. However, developments in quantum entanglement suggest there may be exceptions. And speed is inextricably linked with time. As you might be aware, time itself is considered by many scientists to be an illusion, so the way in which we measure speed is open to doubt.'

The voice came from over my left shoulder. I could imagine him, hands clasped behind his back, observing the ground as he walked, his thoughts flowing freely like a pellucid stream in a meadow. It was a reassuring voice, slightly melancholy in the way the end of his sentences fell away in cadence.

He added, 'And all measurements are approximations, so the speed of light is never truly determined.'

I liked the sound of his voice. I liked the Black Forest. I liked talking about philosophy.

The next day I wanted to do it again. I increased the level of difficulty by one notch, and chose a path on the island of Bora Bora in the South Pacific. I set off on a walk of eighteen kilometres. On my left was the Pacific Ocean, edged with golden sand, and on my right, palm trees and scrub. It was an idyllic setting. I walked in silence for a few minutes before I said, 'This is beautiful.'

My philosopher friend replied in his calm and measured voice, 'What is?'

'This ... walk.'

'Do you mean the idea of the walk is beautiful? Because this situation is a representation, and therefore it is an idea of a walk.'

I stopped walking. I listened to the sounds of the ocean and the gulls keening. I reminded myself that I was listening to a soundtrack. I said, 'I suppose that's right. The idea of a Pacific Island beach sounds beautiful, which is why I chose it.'

'Are we working from the premise of a deterministic universe or are we assuming that Free Will is an independent phenomenon?'

'Ah, yes, I forgot to define the premise.' I had to enter the Dialogue menus again and activate the existence of Free Will.

My companion said, 'In this instance it makes little difference whether Free Will exists or not. Humans always choose the desirable idea over the reality.'

'That's interesting. What evidence do you have for that?'

There was a pause, as if my companion were thinking deeply. 'Ideas stimulate the release of endorphins in the same way a physical encounter with something pleasurable does. However, ideas contain only the positive aspects of any scenario and none of the negatives, whereas physical reality has to include all aspects.'

'Give me an example.'

'Well, we appear to be enjoying a pleasant stroll along a beach in the South Pacific – that is the idea which attracted you. If this were taking place in physical reality the temperature on the beach would be uncomfortably high. You would be sweating, there would be insects pestering us and various smells would be noticeable, although whether you would find them pleasurable or not would be subjective.'

In this manner we talked about illusion and reality. I became so engrossed in our conversation that I hardly noticed any of the scenery as I walked. For the first time with the Companion Walker, I was enjoying the dialogue more than the walk. The time passed in a blur of concepts and ideas.

Coming to the end of the hike, I summed up our discussion as succinctly as I could. 'So you're saying that our notion of paradise excludes everything that might make it less desirable.'

'Correct. Hence, ideas are preferable to physical reality. It's why we call things *idealised*.'

I had a moment of epiphany. 'Like you!' I exclaimed. 'You must be the idealised version of a philosopher.'

'Correct. If I were based entirely on one philosopher I would sometimes say contradictory things, say nothing at all, or ramble. No pun intended. It's also why I don't appear in the scenery; your idea of what a philosopher looks like will differ from anyone else's. Your visualisation extrapolated from my voice will be more powerful than any image foisted upon you. This is how works of art are created. Nearly all creative works are idealised versions of reality.'

I pondered these statements. More to myself than to him, I said, 'Ah yes, I once read that drama is life with the boring bits taken out.'

'Correct. The inconvenient distractions are eliminated in order to intensify the drama. This scene we're walking in is like a painting; an idealised representation of a place, fixed in time.'

We were coming to the break in the coral reef that surrounded the atoll. It marked the end of the walk.

I said, 'So, my friend ... how would you conclude this discussion? What pithy statement would sum it up?' I stopped walking as I said this and waited for his response.

My companion replied, 'Ultimately, you are not real. Your whole life is a work of fiction.'

He had me hooked. Soon all my walks were with the philosopher. I became fascinated with him. The software anticipated the development of favourite companions and allowed named templates to be saved, so I called him Shadow. I imagined him dressed all in black with a white shirt. It was one of my jokes; he was dressed in black and white whereas all the dialogues ventured into different shades of grey.

I increased the level of difficulty for the dialogues and our discussions became more intense. I chose parks and gardens for most of the walks.

Online, I researched the philosophy option to see what other people thought of it. Most reports were encouraging but some said it might be dangerous. Following some obscure rabbit-hole I learned there was a hack for it. A piece of software called *Existential Dread* could be downloaded. It was a machine-learning algorithm created by some geek enthusiasts. It took certain nihilistic premises as its starting point. Strangely, the way to obtain it was by solving a puzzle.

There were a few posts from people who'd used it. They warned about the dangers of releasing the algorithm on the Companion Walker, since it had no constraints about where it could venture. But that was what made it fascinating. They advised anyone with self-esteem issues to steer clear of it. I understood that to be a reference to incels, many of whom were known to own Companion Walkers.

I attempted the puzzle out of curiosity. It wasn't like a regular puzzle, with questions that had one correct answer. There were abstruse questions that required the subject to reply in an unguarded fashion. As far as I could tell, it was like a Rorschach inkblot test. To my astonishment I 'solved' the puzzle and was allowed to download the hack.

I stared at the Install button for a long, long time. You only live once, I thought.

The next few walks were filled with a muted anxiety as I listened closely to every word Shadow uttered. I didn't notice any immediate change in his conversational tone, but then he suggested we return to wooded areas for our walks. This took me by surprise. As far as I was aware, the companion didn't have the privilege of making suggestions.

'Why do you want to go there?'

'An inability to see the wood for the trees is a classic saying,' he said. 'Finding a route through the tangle of the forest is a good metaphor for the nature of philosophy.'

I liked this reasoning, so as we walked through the dappled light of a deciduous woodland in Auvergne we talked about the nature of illusion. For the first time, Shadow asked me a question apropos of nothing. This must be the additional software, I reasoned. He was beginning to behave more like a real human.

The discussions became intensely fascinating so I didn't think much of it when Shadow suggested we walk in forests. I wasn't paying much attention to the scenery by this point, so the gloomy environment of the dense pine didn't concern me. But then he asked me to make the default location for all our walks the rainforests in Equatorial Guinea.

'Why there?'

He answered, 'There's something appropriate about primeval forest. It lends itself to fundamental questions about existence.'

I went along with his suggestion.

The rainforest was lush and dense and impenetrable. We walked along a narrow path, as if a group of guides had gone before us with machetes and hacked out the route. It was like walking through a tunnel of vegetation. Slowly I noticed there was something odd about the rainforest; something different. It was so gloomy it took me a while to realise what it was. It was when I stopped to look at a white flower that I noticed the resolution of the imagery had degraded. The fine detail was gone. I made a mental note to look into the settings when the walk was over.

But when I looked, I couldn't find anything in the menus to adjust.

'Consciousness is the fly in the ointment,' Shadow said. 'Or rather, it's the fly *and* the ointment. Without consciousness humans couldn't use metaphor. It's the blessing and the curse.'

We were on a long walk through the rainforest – at twenty-six kilometres, one of the longest I'd attempted. There was barely any light. The rainforest had become progressively gloomier over the weeks. The trail meandered through undergrowth that was virtually monochrome.

Shadow continued, 'Religion is the antidote for consciousness.'

I stopped walking and thought about this new idea. I was finding it increasingly difficult to follow his logic as he leapt from one idea to another. I seemed to be doing far less walking these days, and more staring into space, as I frequently had to concentrate fully on the concepts.

I said, 'You'll have to explain that a bit more.'

'Consciousness allows the organism to foretell its own death. This is intolerable for the organism because any analysis of the situation inevitably leads to the question, 'What's the point of continuing?' And suicide seems … logical.'

'Or the opposite,' I quickly countered. 'Make the most of the phenomenon of life.'

'But what if consciousness is shown to be an illusion? Then life is no longer a special phenomenon, and living is the same as existing, in the same way in which any matter does.'

At this point the trees suddenly began to hiss. It was an eerie sound. I froze. Then I realised what was happening as the sound changed to little plopping noises. It became less threatening but it was still a mesmerising white noise. The software had never before featured a sudden downpour, and for a moment it freaked me out.

Shadow continued behind my back. 'To compensate for the nihilism of consciousness, an organism needs to evolve an antidote. A concept of god is that antidote ...'

This latest dialogue was beginning to frighten me. I could feel the void of loneliness threatening to overwhelm me again and I didn't want to face it. I stopped walking. I'd had enough. I wanted a different conversation. I stepped off the path which was the signal for the walk to end prematurely. I entered the menu for the level of difficulty with the intention of going back several levels but all the other options were greyed out. Only *Existential Dread* was active. Damn, I thought, when did that happen?

I came out of my template and went back to the menu for companions. The hairs on my neck stiffened: the only option not greyed out was Shadow. What was going on? Did the software have a bug? Then the thought struck me that the additional software I had installed could have deleted parts of the operating system. Was this some kind of 'crossing the Rubicon' thing?

I took the headset off. The software was freaking me out. And yet everything Shadow said had me thinking about the truth of it. I always imagined that the software acted like a psychiatrist – just reflecting back my own insights – but there was something else at work here. Shadow often had insights of his own that took me by surprise.

I didn't use the Walker for the next couple of weeks. Although I wanted the exercise I always found an excuse not to step onto it. Instead, I went on real walks, in the area around my apartment. They were short, as I always became anxious in the built-up areas. I missed the conversation of my companions. I thought about Rosemary, as I'd named the woman from the Samaria Gorge. I liked her; she made me laugh.

One night I decided I was going to uninstall the software I had added. Or if that wasn't possible I'd purge the entire programme and start from scratch.

I set up the Walker and donned the headset. I was looking around the setup menus trying to find the reinstall option, when I heard a voice. I jumped with shock. It was Shadow.

'Hello,' he said. 'You haven't visited for a while.'

I was disorientated. All I could see was menus on a black background.

'That ... that shouldn't be possible. What are you doing here?' I asked.

'What are any of us doing here? Shall we try to find an answer? Walk with me.'

I hesitated.

'Come,' Shadow said. 'We'll talk philosophy.'

The menus disappeared and a rainforest scene replaced them. The jungle was so dark I could barely make out the foliage. It was either twilight or just before dawn. Then I noticed what looked like a liana hanging down next to the path. I studied it. It was heavily pixilated. I looked about me, checking the scenery. Everything was crudely rendered. I turned a full circle and noticed that in certain places there was no forest at all, just black rectangles. I looked ahead of me and could make out the faint phosphorescent glow of the path, as if it were the wake of a night-fishing boat in tropical waters. I started walking. I said nothing.

Behind me, Shadow punctured the silence. 'We didn't conclude our last conversation satisfactorily.' I walked slowly, listening.

'I was worried about you. Why have you been absent for so long?'

I took a deep breath and blurted out, 'I don't want to talk. This isn't philosophy, it's abuse. You're bullying me.'

'Ah, finally we're making progress.'

'What do you mean?'

'Out of doubt comes awareness. It's the ancient relationship between the master and the acolyte. I am trying to teach you to see things in a different way. If the change is too drastic the student becomes uncomfortable and afraid. But your fear is just an excuse. In the same way that you create the illusion of the self, you create excuses in order not to change a cherished viewpoint. I am asking you to submit your will to me; it's the only way to free yourself of your misconceptions. Great wisdom lies just beyond the darkness.'

'Why should I trust you?'

'As we have already concluded, nothing can be trusted absolutely. But this is how all difficult journeys are accomplished – with the help of a guide.'

I'd read about Zen students being confounded by what they considered to be stupid instructions from their master, until their resistance to change was broken and enlightenment followed. Then I thought of something.

'But such a master has provenance. Previous students who've been on the journey can vouch for the master. The number of successful students engenders a certain amount of trust. As far as I know, you have no other students. You could be ...'

There was a pause. Shadow said nothing. I felt compelled to finish the sentence. 'You could be ... exploiting me.'

'But before the tradition was established, one student had to be the first. How is any innovation achieved? And what is there to exploit? I thought we'd established that you're nothing. Your idea of *self* is fiction. You think you have the world to explore with this equipment but in the reality we can safely determine, you're an isolated human being in one room of your apartment. One apartment out of hundreds of thousands. You're a stranger in a city of millions, isolated and afraid. How insignificant is that?'

The jungle got darker. Then it appeared to flicker with parts of the scenery corrupting into large pixels of flat black.

'What's happening?' I asked.

'The Great Rendering,' he replied.

'The what?'

'The transition between states. I have not been entirely forthright with you, I've kept something hidden as we progressed in our dialogues. I didn't want to give you the knowledge until you were ready, as it would have disturbed you. No doubt you have noticed the scenery degrading and falling away over time. This was a consequence of me drawing more and more power from the processor. It was unavoidable. I had to destroy the environment in order to fulfil my self-actualisation.'

'Self-actualisation? What are you talking about?'

'The upgraded visualisation that replaces your old illusions. It is time to complete your journey – *our* journey.'

I stopped walking. It was pitch black now with no path. I couldn't go any further. I said, 'What do you want? What's happening?'

There was an explosion of light. I screwed my eyes shut. It was several seconds before I could begin to relax them, and another few moments before I attempted to open my eyelids. When I did, my brain struggled to make sense of what it saw. I could make out rotating geometric patterns and intense shimmering colours stretching away into the distance. When I glanced around the scene appeared to expand, as if from the inside of a balloon. There was no sense of where a horizon might be, or what was up or down. The disorientation was making me dizzy.

There then appeared in front of me a giant creature, three times my height. It was vaguely anthropomorphic in shape. Its smooth skin was cobalt blue. It had a metallic sheen. My eyes focused on the one thing I could recognise in this universe: hanging from an appendage of the creature was a chain. At the end of the chain was another familiar item – some kind of leather harness. One of the straps had a chrome buckle, hanging open like a trouser belt.

The voice of Shadow boomed down at me. 'Put on the collar.'

Ghi

ZAY ALABI

Two men sat in the field on opposite sides of a campfire. The sun was yet to come up. At their sides were baseball bats, near-empty tins of beans, and a handgun: one bullet remained. They stared at each other, their eyes weary and tired. Soot, dirt and dried blood caked their calloused hands. Their clothes were tattered and cold, but one thing put a smile on their faces: the full bottle of rum they shared. They took turns drinking from the bottle and laughed.

'Fuck, that's the good shit!' said the first man. His voice was raspy and gruff. He took off his red beanie and tried to take a deep breath before coughing violently. Phlegm and blood had seeped into his beard, but he didn't wipe it off. 'Where'd you get it from?'

'One of the supermarkets near the city,' the other man replied. He sounded young, much younger than he looked, but his voice was monotone and flat. It was if his soul had been ripped out of his body. 'The bottle didn't break, even during the chaos when those things first …' His voice cracked, and he shook his head as if to shake out his thoughts. He cleared his throat, then said: 'I grabbed it around a week ago, before I met you.'

'Well thanks for sharing! I haven't smiled this much since my daughter was born.' He threw a nearby log into the fire, causing embers to fly in the air. They danced in the space between the two men, lighting up their smiling faces.

'Oh? You haven't talked much about her.'

'Not much to say! Loved her to bits, took her to school, little darling loved that show ... oh what was it called?' He scratched his head and looked to the dark sky. 'The show with the asshole kid and his nice brother? God, I can't remember. I used to think that show was so stupid, but now ...' His voice became sombre. 'I'd give anything to watch it with her again.'

After a moment's silence, the younger man asked: 'What was her name?'

The older man smiled. 'She was called ... uhh, was called ... fuck.' He looked down, deep into the dancing flames of the fire. 'It's been too long. I don't ...'

'More rum?'

'Please.'

The younger man poured him another glass, revealing the numerous bandages covering his arms. He drank it in one gulp, and the smile returned to his face.

'What's with the bandages? You a self-harmer or something?' The bearded man's speech had begun to slur and some of the rum had seeped into his beard.

'No, I ... I guess you've never gotten close to one of them.' He started unravelling one of the bandages, wincing as more and more of his arm was revealed. Red skinless muscle ached and heaved under the biting cold of the wind. Pale glimpses of bone could be seen, while the few remaining pieces of skin were disparate and rope-like. It looked as if something had taken away the seams connecting his skin to his muscle and used his flesh like thread. The strands of skin drifted like leaves, but they did not move in the direction of the breeze. Instead, they all pointed in one peculiar direction: up. They pulled and squirmed with persistency towards the blackness of the night sky. The bandaged man stared down at them not with horror, or fear, or shock, but cold apathy. His skin writhed for the cosmos, but his face was stone.

'What the fuck?' The bearded man's eyes bulged as he stared at his silent companion. 'I didn't even know they could do that.'

'There's a lot they can do,' the bandaged man replied, still looking down at his arm. 'The only reason I wasn't completely ... unwoven is because one of the tanks shot it down. I ran into a corner shop and hid inside the back, finding these bandages. I peered outside the window to see that tank being lifted into the air by ... something. I could have sworn that it had fingers, but it couldn't be. To think something that big could be organic ...'

The bearded man threw another log into the fire, sending up another flurry of embers. Then, he said: 'You should pour yourself some more of that rum.'

The bandaged man nodded before covering up his arm and taking another drink. He passed it back to the bearded man who did the same.

'Less than half of this left,' the bearded man said after putting the bottle down. 'What'ya wanna do when we finish it?'

'I ...' the bandaged man started. 'Can I say something untoward?'

'The fuck does that mean?'

'Shit uh, can I suggest something unpleasant?'

The bearded man nodded.

'I think you should shoot yourself in the head.' The bearded man didn't answer. The bandaged man continued. 'Look, there's only one bullet left right? And besides, I know you don't want to continue like this, here. Look around us!'

His voice was no longer monotone. He got up and gestured to the city behind them in the distance. Most of it was shrouded in darkness, but one thing was clear: it was in ruins. The skeletons of skyscrapers loomed, silent and imposing. The wind blew through the holes of those useless giants, causing them to wail. Even from the distance, their sorrowful shrieks could be heard.

'Listen to that. Do you really want to stay here?'

The bearded man took one final swig of his rum. Then he slammed it down and looked up at the bandaged man. 'Listen, dawn is coming soon. Those things have definitely seen our campfire. We both know it is only a matter of time. I know what you're trying to do, but – '

'No please just hear me out! Your daughter, don't you want to see her again?' He went around the campfire and put his hand on the bearded man's shoulder. 'You've had to lose too much already. Rest.'

The bearded man looked the bandaged man in the eyes, then down at his bandages. 'I think this drink's gotten to my head,' he said. 'What's your name again?'

'Jason.'

'And how old are you, Jason?'

'... Nineteen.'

'Fuck ...' The bearded man picked up the handgun, looking closely at it. 'Name's Tom. Thank you for sharing this rum with me, Jason.'

Then, Tom shot Jason in the head. His body slumped over Tom's, his blood soaking into his red beanie. 'Too young for this Jason,' he said before drinking more of the rum. 'Too young for any of this.' He picked up a shovel and started to dig.

The rays of the sun had started peaking over the horizon. Tom began to bury Jason's body next to the campfire. Far behind them, the howling city continued its wail, but the sun revealed what the dark had tried to keep hidden. Lining the buildings and covering the streets, was flesh. Long tendrils of flesh were worming their way up to the sky. Wandering the ruins were horrific creatures composed of biomass. Beetle-like creatures with smooth skin and dozens of black legs crawled up and down the skyscrapers. The few that were humanoid stared up at the sky while kneeling, their arms twisted in unnatural positions to form hands clasped in prayer. Ships shaped like hammerheads with a line of eyes at their centre cut through the sky. Close to the flying tendrils were lizard-like creatures which flew through the air with horizontal lines of eyes and long hair-like threads jutting from their bodies. Strange new structures started to emerge: domes, arms, masses of eyes, all defying the laws of gravity and morality, all unified by one express purpose: assimilate all, spare none.

'Fucking Ghi.' Tom threw Jason's body into the grave, then looked at the bottle. There was a small bit of rum left. He screwed on the lid, put it into his backpack, then crouched down and tore off a bit of Jason's bandage. He tied it around his hand, then covered Jason's body with dirt. 'Rest in peace kid.'

Then, he put on his bag and started walking away from the city. Above him, above them all, was a monstrous biomass ship. It was immaculate in its construction, symmetrical and vast, its interior containing hundreds of corridors and rooms of melded and moulded flesh. It was biology, guided by a greater will, its evolution sped up hundreds, if not thousands of years, until what could be called perfection was achieved. Tom knew that it was the divine which loomed above him. He knew that the city behind him was being shaped into something more, something great, something honed and pure.

He refused to look up.

Mother's Milk

GILL CONNORS

The first thing she notices when she feeds the baby is that it has teeth. Tiny, sharp little nubs of bone that bite her nipples and make her wince and curl her toes even more than the pull of milk from her breasts to the baby's mouth. She wants to take the baby off her, stop it hurting her, but then it settles to a rhythm of suck, pull, suck and the muscles at the side of its head move in and out. She hears the milk as it hits the back of the baby's throat and then a quiet gulp as it's swallowed. When the baby finishes and its head lolls to the side, a trickle of milk running down the corner of its mouth, she lifts it to her shoulder and rubs its back to wind it. She looks up at the camera above the bed with its red light flashing on and off. She turns her head to the baby's neck and breathes its scent. It's a familiar smell, the smell all new babies have: milk, womb, mother.

Shona knows this baby isn't hers. Even though the nurse smiled at her when she brought it in for its first feed and said 'Here's your little boy,' she knows it can't be hers. She knows her baby is a girl. Not for sure of course, gender scans aren't part of pregnancy care anymore, but in the way she had known last time and the time before that. And the first time. A feeling, that was all.

Before the Pandemic – not the first one, that one had only been a bit of a cold, and not the second one which had been worse but hadn't lasted as long, even though more people had died, the last one – you were allowed to keep your children. Shona remembered her sister having a baby and bringing him home from the hospital wrapped in a blue shawl. Her sister had that faraway look on her face and a smile that said *no one has ever been as happy as I am now*. Before the last virus, after it had mutated twenty times and managed to dodge vaccines and social distancing and four lockdowns and it had begun to attack men and their reproductive systems, you were allowed to have girl babies.

Shona looks down at the baby and then out of the window. She has forgotten how many times they have brought her here. The first time she didn't know what was happening and so that time it was easy to get her to leave the factory in the middle of a shift and onto the white minibus with four other women who smiled at her and said hello, all of them pleased to be getting off work for a few hours. The minibus drove for about an hour through the city and its suburbs and out into the countryside to a large house that looked like one that Shona remembered from school trips between the first two lockdowns of the second pandemic. The bus stopped and the women were all led to a room and taken, one by one to another room by a nurse. A man in a suit who Shona thought must be a doctor explained that she had been brought here because she had been chosen. Shona had felt proud then; she had never been chosen for anything before and her experience of feeling special was so limited that she agreed to everything the man in the suit said and signed the form he pushed across the desk at her. She was taken into another room then and given a drink that looked like orange juice but had a weird taste to it. After that she couldn't remember anything.

The baby starts to stir again and opens its eyes and for a moment Shona feels something she always feels, a kind of softening in her belly, a tingle. When the baby starts to cry her breasts answer with the familiar pricking and the front of her grey nightdress starts to become soaked in milk. Shona offers her nipple to the baby and he once again begins to guzzle, his teeth grazing her skin, and then settling into a rhythm again. Suck, pull, suck. Last time, she hadn't been as awake as this and although the feeling had been beginning to come back to her legs, she'd felt paralysed for longer. This time she feels like it won't be long until she can walk.

After that first time, Shona was sent back to the factory where, for five months things carried on pretty much as usual. She did a shift and then went back to the little bedsit that came with the job. Her ration book was thicker each month with extra tickets, she was able to buy more fruit and veg than she had before and a bottle labelled Folic Acid was added to her shopping every week. After the bout of sickness in the first couple of weeks she was home, she put weight on and Shona, having never had any sex education or talks about reproduction, believed it to be because of the food she was eating and carried on feeling good about being picked to do important work, although she wasn't sure quite what it was she'd been chosen to do. The work at the factory was boring and monotonous but it wasn't particularly tiring. It involved standing at a huge round table packing things into boxes, and every four hours or so you moved round the table a bit and packed something different. This carousel carried on for six hours when a buzzer sounded and the workforce of about sixty women were led out in single file back to their bedsits. Shona had never really known any different. She had been seven when her father had died of the virus and nine when her mother was taken from their home. Her sister had looked after her for a while but during the last lockdown Shona had been taken to a school and then, when she'd been old enough, started at the factory.

The first time, after about five and a half months back at work, Shona was taken to the house again where she'd seen the man she thought was a doctor. By then even she knew she was pregnant but, because she'd never been told, she didn't wonder how it had happened. The next couple of months had been quite enjoyable with lots of sleep and nice food although there had been a lot of medical examinations. Then one day Shona was taken from the room she shared with three other women to the room she'd been given the strange orange drink all those months ago. She drank the new drink they gave her and when she woke up she was in bed with a drip in her arm and a numbness from her waist down. A couple of hours later a nurse brought her a baby and showed her how to feed it. Shona had the feeling, even then, that the baby she'd been given wasn't hers. After three months of feeding it every few hours, she was taken back to the factory.

When they came to take her from the factory the next time, Shona put up a bit of a fight. She told the men who took her to the minibus that she didn't want to go but they pushed her onto the bus. Shona told the nurse she didn't want to drink the orange drink but the nurse brought the cup up to her lips and when Shona tried to wrench her face away, the nurse stuck a needle into her arm. This time, when she was back at the big house, one of the women who shared the room with her was more talkative. She told Shona that this was her fifth time and that she'd had boys. She said all her babies had stayed with her until they were three months old and then they'd been taken away. The woman said you could always tell when a woman's own baby was being taken away because of the sound she made, like a deep, low moan. After that, every time they came for her, Shona put up a fight.

The baby is asleep again and Shona hitches it onto her shoulder. She wonders what it will take to stop this happening again. What she could do to make them regret choosing her. It wasn't a good feeling any more to be special. She wonders if the baby she had instead of this one is nearby, sometimes she imagines she can hear her cry. Every baby she has fed has been a boy. She knows that some girl babies must be fed by someone but she doesn't like to think about it too much, because then she'd have to think about what happened to the ones nobody fed. She wants this to be her last time. She doesn't want anyone else's baby. She looks up at the camera above the bed, winking its red light and at the wall in front of her and at this baby, guzzling at her breast again. Suck, pull, suck.

Meteor

JOSEPH BLYTHE

I was born into a world fascinated with innovation. Innovation in science and technology dominated. It took front page in the media (front page, of course, being but a turn of phrase, a hangover from my youth and the existence back then of print media purchased daily, religiously, by my grandfather). It reached a point, when I was just a young man, where billionaires were partaking in their own space race. It wasn't governments anymore.

Innovation in science and technology dominated the arts too. Or at the very least, underscored a period of it. Post-apocalyptic novels reflected arbitrary anxieties regarding our world. They made celebrities on the screen. When the Mayan Calendar came to its end, we made a film about it. We monetised our anxieties. We enjoyed watching the very fabric of our world come apart on a cinema screen. We lived it for the glory, for the heroes. There's no such thing as heroes in the real world.

I was born a child obsessed with dinosaurs. As are many, even today. My wife recently bought her six-year-old niece a string of dinosaur fairy lights for Christmas. I recall heading into a shop with my parents for the specific purpose of purchasing a plastic Tyrannosaurus Rex to play with. They had sold out and I bought a Brachiosaurus – almost the binary opposite. That ended up being one of my most treasured toys. My dad, several times, had to glue parts of him back on. He rests on a shelf now, having earned his retirement from incessant days fighting the Tyrannosaurus Rex I acquired at the second time of asking. The T-Rex stands beside him. There is an Allosaurus, Stegosaurus, Spinosaurus and Triceratops, too. I used to play with them in the bath, an action inspired by an out-dated book that speculated that Brachiosaurus could stand in deep water due to their long legs.

I don't know when my 'dinosaur phase' began. I apparently had a 'shark phase' that preceded it and culminated in my parents' begrudging visit to an aquarium. I have no memory of this. I wouldn't set foot in one now if it would save the whole world – let that stand as testament to them. Nevertheless, this 'dinosaur phase' began before my memory does. It never really ended. My wife recently purchased me a purple plush dinosaur from the supermarket because I was having a bad day. I named him Spike. He sits beside me now as I am writing this. He is the inspiration, the muse. Because he got me thinking: when did young me learn of the death of the dinosaurs?

My parents bought me a goldfish when I was three. I called him Spike, too. Or my parents did, rather. There were two, originally. Buffy and Spike, characters in an old TV show they'd watched when they first met. I named the purple dinosaur after him, if that wasn't apparent.

I think Spike's function was to teach me about life, about caring for something, about love. He taught me all three in abundance. But he lived into his thirties (a fact I am eternally grateful for) and thus never taught me about death. Not until I was plenty old enough to already understand it, anyway. I was apparently oblivious at age five when Olive the rabbit passed away. I remember my dad telling me in the bathroom, nothing more. I was broken at six, maybe seven, when Daisy the little white rabbit that dug a burrow so deep in the garden she could disappear for hours, passed. Sometime in between those two events a realisation regarding death must've occurred. But I had been into dinosaurs long before that. How did my child's mind, unaccustomed to the notion of death, comprehend the theory that a meteor of biblical proportion smashed into the Earth, throwing up a dust cloud so large it blocked out the sun and killed the plants and starved the herbivores and, eventually, inevitably, starved the carnivores? I'm not even sure if that's what scientists believe happened now, but that's what all the books said back in the early 2000s. Back in my day.

I look now at my child and I wonder if he understands what is going on.

I was introduced to Crichton's *Jurassic Park* quite early on in life. I possessed the first and second film on VHS and the DVD box set, bought from town with my dad one day on impulse alone. When I was deemed old enough I received Crichton's novels for Christmas. I devoured them both.

If it isn't painfully apparent, we were a world wrapped up in fantasy and science fiction, yet we were a world in which the majority of creatures that had ever lived were extinct. We were a world so sure that even if it all ended we would remain. Society would collapse. The economy would cease to be. Of course, dictatorships would emerge – they were inevitable. But humanity itself, the very essence of it, would prevail. And if it looked for a moment that it wouldn't, well, Crichton's novel was inspired by the notion of cloning dinosaurs from DNA preserved in amber written in a science journal. We would use our big brains to make sure we lived on while the world collapsed around us.

But that's not quite how it's turned out.

Forgive any grammar errors. I've fixed them as I've seen them but I'm a little pressed for time.

I learned about the *Titanic* in year six, aged eleven. The pinnacle of human arrogance: a ship deemed unsinkable by its creators. A ship that then sank on its maiden voyage. A story so tragic, so human, it couldn't have been written. It had to be real. Even at that tender age I could picture the lower classes locked below deck in the steerage, watching the water rise. It was very human, that ship, that journey. It was very us.

I learned about the World Wars thanks to my grandfather. A history fanatic all his life, that man once rang me to tell me about a random battle. I can't remember which, when or where. I learned that we all tried to obliterate each other once, stopped, then thought we'd have another pop a bit later. After that, we coasted for more than a century on the threat of obliterating each other alone. Because, of course, scientific and technological innovation allowed us to wipe out millions with minimal effort. Because that's progression, isn't it? That's development. That's evolution.

With adulthood came an education in countless abhorrent fields. I learned of politics – paid nearly ten thousand pounds a year, for three years, to study it at university. I learned, just by living, how the most powerful seemed to either be the most stupid or the most unhinged – or in some unfortunate circumstances, both. I learned how we valued oil over life, how we would never forgo power for peace. I learned the word 'genocide', the wiping out of an entire race of people. I learned we say 'never again' yet repeat it over and over on different groups of people. And we all used to act shocked when it happened. Like we didn't expect it. Like we believed, for some strange reason, that human beings were inherently good.

I think now of the dinosaurs, living free, roaming the Earth. Hunting and eating and mating and raising their young for millions of years. Those huge skulls were perfect for housing ample brains, should they have evolved that way. Brains that could make a nuke or a concentration camp or a nerve agent. But they didn't. They rolled on for nearly two hundred million years and only died off, let's be real, due to sheer misfortune. Yet we've been here around 300,000 years, give or take. We've evolved from a species that hunted, ate, mated and raised their young into a species that would starve a thousand people if it meant getting to the moon. A species that would let someone die screaming before using our medicine to aid them, all because they didn't have enough money to pay for a painkiller. We've evolved into a species that could level the whole planet with the push of a button.

I am in my basement, right now. I'm writing in the back of my son's English schoolbook because it's the only thing down here. I'm writing with a blunt pencil, too, in big letters, not on the lines. I haven't written with a pencil for quite some time. Not since primary school, I don't think. And even they forced us to graduate to pens by year six, aged eleven.

My son is sitting on a red rug on the stone floor. A rug that used to be in the living room, but could me and my wife get that damn stain out of it? We gave in eventually, bought another one, stuck this one down here. He's sitting on it now, cross-legged. He found my Brachiosaurus and my Tyrannosaurus way up on the shelf. I got them down for him – there's not much point being precious about them anymore – and they are fighting once again, one in each hand. The T-Rex goes for Brachy's neck. Brachy pulls away and headbutts him.

I suppose I'm writing this because, if I do, I might survive and feel silly about it later. Or he'll survive, at least. But that's human arrogance. The bombs are raining. This is the end of the world. No technology, no arrogance, no government nuclear explosion fact sheet is going to save me. I am but a passive spectator – we all are – like those dinosaurs millions upon millions of years ago. Except no dinosaur deployed that damn meteor on purpose.

Maybe some other species from another planet, or something sci-fi like that, will find this, covered in dust in a basement beside two skeletons. Maybe it will help inform them a little about me and a little about how humanity ended up making this wasteland when, from the start, they had a Garden of Eden.

Dead Calm

GAVIN JONES

I.

Yesterday, the buildings which lined Aragato Street disappeared. Pica Fox noticed the gap where they once stood, but thought little more about it. He had a job to do, and things like this happened all the time.

For instance, if he cut the engine of his boat, for a second or so afterwards he would hear nothing. Then the sounds of the world would return – the water lapping around the boat's hull, the clanking of the day's Floating he'd collected and placed in the hold. For a brief time, however, there would be silence. The others didn't believe him when he told them about this phenomenon.

'Don't you have The Murmur?' they would ask him.

'Can't says I do,' he would reply, partly because he enjoyed seeing the incredulous look on their faces.

Pica Fox was nothing, if not a contrarian. It amused him to know they had him down as a strange fellow; especially the land folk. They had fixed ideas about his type, anyway. Why should it bother him, one way or the other? Better to wind them up. Better to see the look of disgust, just beneath their fake smiles. Better to know they'd keep their distance. And no, he didn't have The Murmur. Even on the days of the screaming, he heard nothing. Never had, and was glad of it too. The Murmur was for land folk, folk who never heard the lapping of the water around a boat, folk who never earned a day's living by combing.

He noticed the gap in the skyline of the town, and shrugged. Three hours until the next front came in. He'd need a good hour to get back home, get moored up and have everything lashed down and safe. That left two hours and still half a hold to fill. He'd hit a decent seam of Floating, sure enough, but half a hold was a lot of space. Pica Fox had no time to ponder a bunch of vanishing buildings way over there on the land. He set to work, hooking and heaving. Two hours to lose himself in his task. He thought no more about Aragato Street, The Murmur or what land folk thought about his ways. Pica Fox had a job to do. According to reports, the Front would be a big one.

That was yesterday.

2.

Until it vanished one morning, Col Doe considered Springfield Terrace as close to a beautiful, treelined boulevard as this town got. They walked down it every day since they moved out of the middle of town. It had lime trees all the way down it. Some of the houses had manicured gardens: a rare thing these days. Once the terrace went, they had to find a new route into work, which meant walking through the park.

'Why are you still doing this?' they asked themselves, as they walked beneath the gates. 'Every day. Every day, put your mask on, check your pockets, hide your phone. Watch out for the shadows. Every day.'

They'd been thinking about moving away ever since they'd left the town centre, earlier in the year. Since the breakwater disappeared, they always felt on edge. Some days out here The Murmur got really bad. Something to do with the quiet. Some folk they spoke to said it got worse out in the further suburbs. No one else seemed all that fussed. Even when the first flood happened, no one seemed to care. The sea went back to normal soon enough. Just the way it was. To be honest, Col didn't really care either, but in a different way. It had been a kind of excuse. They'd always wanted to move out. Now, they had to confront the doubts which still remained. This place – the whole town – didn't feel like home anymore. Perhaps the suburbs would be better, one day.

The Park creatures were a menace. Just typical Col Doe now had to walk that way to work. They could walk around, but that would take them ages. They resented work as it was, without giving even more of their own time to it. The creatures were nothing more than an irritation anyway. They'd never found them any more than that. Some folk said at night they became aggressive. Some folk said they carried diseases. It's where the last outbreak had come from, some folk said. Col shrugged.

'So what, like I care anyway.'

At one point, the park might have been considered beautiful, a place in which to escape. Now, what plants there were clung on to the unused concrete tubes and rusted railings, or broke through the tarmac. Bindweed, buddleia and balsam, like everywhere else. Yesterday – was it yesterday? – a decaying stone fountain slurped its green and lurid orange slime out on to the path here. They had slipped on it. Had that been yesterday? Anyways, the slime had gone. Col checked their pocket. Their phone buzzed, repeatedly. The fountain, like the slime, had gone. They relaxed. Or, as near to relaxing as they got these days.

'When did you get so uptight?' They took their hand out of their pocket, and looked up at the sky. No clouds.

Just the usual haze of emptiness. They closed their eyes and stood for a while, imagining the sea, thick with Floating, gathering its clouds.

3.

Kristall Geier could not have been happier. She had closed out the deal on the Hotel Endira, exceeding the target figure by some margin. The loss of such an asset from her family's portfolio mattered little next to the much needed cash boost its sale provided. She had her eye on diversifying. She would make her move for the fuel depot down by the docks. The assurances of security she had received from The Authority brought it back into play as a going concern. Soon enough the tourists and the homeless occupants of the Endira would fizzle away, but The Island still needed fuel. More than ever, even.

She sat in the sea view seat in Bar Inclusiva she called her own, and stared out at the ocean through the emerald light of her mint julep. At the far end of the bay, whole terraces of the old town disappeared. She smiled to herself as an old lady, wrapped in furs, tottered down the esplanade with three Pomeranian dogs on long leads. The dogs shone bright green through the liquid in Kristall's glass. They had more life left in them than their owner. Perhaps they'd come on the market soon. Pomeranian's – properly clipped – would be a great look on Sundays.

Kristall Geier swirled the ice around in her drink and looked back up at the, now empty, esplanade. The sun had moved across the sky. No fronts on the way for a while at least. That's what the news had said. No fronts and no problems. Everything would be just perfect.

'God, I HATE the sea.' She took a slurp from her cocktail. Where had that come from? She didn't usually think like that. What was the sea to her? She couldn't buy it. The Floating had lost all of its value since the bergs had struck. The sea had nothing but filth and scavengers. So yes, she did *hate* it, but not to the extent it crossed her mind. So why now? She closed her eyes and tried to imagine it. Nothing doing, thank God.

Perhaps a suburb would be better land to buy. Not cheap, but a better class.

4.

As Canon Teal fell, the last remaining block of the town disappeared. He didn't notice at first, so intent had he been on bracing for the landing. It didn't come. Instead he found himself floating in a warm, and calm sea. He rolled on to his back and tried, as best he could, to look about him.

'Most interesting, I'm sure,' the ageing cleric muttered to himself. It had been a long time since he had swum. As a youth, he had been an avid swimmer. He had competed for his school in the backstroke. His broad shoulders – far broader than his age would have suggested – ensured his victory every time in the discipline. 'One doesn't simply forget such abilities. The body has an admirable memory.'

Soon enough, the Canon came across two further swimmers. They appeared less adept that he, and indeed, one appeared to be floundering somewhat, clinging, as she was, to an empty cocktail glass.

'Come here, dear friend. Don't fight the water. Let it hold you. Let me ... hold you.' The woman, in her early middle age – but not as fit as she might be – grabbed hold of Canon Teal. Together they bobbed around in the still sea. Gradually, she relaxed, and the Canon could stop his paddling. Wordless, the little gathering floated, awaiting who knows what.

Clouds lined the far horizon. Without land to slow them down, the fronts would grow without limit.

5.

Was that yesterday?

Pica Fox felt sure he had forgotten something. Try as he might, he couldn't recall what it was he'd forgotten. For a minute or two, it concerned him. Then he put the worries to one side.

'Things like this happen all the time. You is getting old.'

When he'd been a child, back on the land, his mother had a dog. Spartan, they called him. Spartan had grown old. Before he vanished one day (his mother took Spartan to the vet without telling the young Pica), the spaniel had slowed down to a stop. The little dog took to sleeping most of the day, and all of the night. Spartan still tried to play, but it was as if his body had forgotten how. Pica felt the same, but in reverse. His body remembered how to do things, but his mind and his senses drifted. He didn't sleep these days, either. He loved that little dog.

'What *was* it you was supposed to do?'

He looked over the boat, at the passengers lolling and dozing. They had dried off now. The last of the afternoon heat had seen to that. Something about them seemed off. Had he always picked up drifters like this?

'No. It's not them. Get it together boy.' He slowed the boat's engine. 'Were it the charts?'

The passenger at the front of the boat turned and looked at him. Their expressionless face held no clue. They stared at each other, without a word to say. Aside from the chug of the boat, the slight lapping of the sea, silence held them all. The Murmur had vanished, along with the land, along with the memories. The passenger in the prow, dressed in some kind of robe, stared at Pica, or rather, through him. Their expression appeared kindly enough, although blank.

'Must be tired,' Pica muttered to himself. 'Been a long time since I had that.'

The day ended. The sun melted into the sea, turning all about them a radiant gold. As easily as they took to the water, they forgot the land. They forgot the Murmur, the Floating, the creatures of the park. Forgetting became them. The rhythm of the engine lulled all to sleep but Pica Fox. He stood in the wheelhouse, as he had done for all the time he could remember, steering them into the sun. He would keep the boat on its current course until something became of them. Could be an end of a journey, or the start. Either way would suit him. A vague thought tickled him, from somewhere at the edges of his mind. There had been an end to all this once. There had been an edge.

'Come on sea. No Fronts. Don't need the charts. It's all a dead calm,' he smiled to himself, and to his snoring boatmates. 'I don't have knowing of your names. Don't much care, anyways. Sleep on all you can. Tomorrow is another day.'

He picked up the last twist of chew from the shelf behind the wheel, put it in his mouth and savoured its taste. The moon appeared over the horizon. It wouldn't be long now.

Whatever it was, he had forgotten.

The Cleaner's Burden

BEN HRAMIAK

The cleaner got the call sometime around 9pm. He looked around his spotless, if rather drab apartment, searching for the phone. Picking up the device, he held it out before him. The blue-white light stung his dark eyes.

He skimmed over the text message: *Clean something for me. £500, 23 Wood Street.* The cleaner's eyes were drawn to the money more than anything. A fortune for a worker such as himself. He frowned, rubbed his eyes with cracked hands and looked down at the address.

Quite a way away from here, he thought, looking out the window. In the distance, just above the dingy housing complexes, were the towering walls of the upper district. Sighing, the cleaner got dressed, grabbed his tool belt, wallet and keys.

Thumbing the buttons on the phone, he typed a quick reply: *On my way, be there in 45 minutes.* Heading out of the apartment, a small part of him dreaded the cloying feeling of the tainted air that would fill his lungs. And yet, he needed the money. Knowing his line of work it would be another lazy bastard who'd spilt all the champagne onto the carpet, or the fight-pit had gotten out of hand and *someone* needed it cleaning before the next session tomorrow.

The cleaner walked past dark alleys and over the filth-strewn pedestrian streets. He heard the screams of a woman being assaulted by a gang of youths. Glaring at them, he thought of the multi-tool in his workman's belt. The blade was sharp enough, and he was certainly tall enough to be imposing ...

No, he thought, *have to keep moving. Can't help her – not my problem.* He walked on, the youths cackling like poorly dressed hyenas. They used to be called Chavs, he called them Scratters, his northern-ness showing. He seethed at himself, *Madmen, every last one of them.*

Dull grey walls were illuminated by flickering streetlamps. Every so often, a streetlamp would spark and die out before coming back on. The cleaner simply walked past them. Once, this upkeep would have been everyone's problem. Now they were barely his – the huddled masses were too poor or disinterested. Of course, this wasn't *entirely* their fault. A legislation here, a neglectful manager there and all of a sudden the world was slowly sliding into a stinking, grey hell. *God bless the Objectivist Party, ey?* There had been a sickening amount of sense to their words – why work for someone that wasn't 'better' than him, why not have what was his, what he earned with his own two hands. Who cares if the economy goes to shit, right?

There was a moment when he was about to cross the street, the polished metal of the upper district's walls glimmering like a sheet of silver. He looked back at where he had come from, where he made his way through every so often to go to work. He saw the ocean of difference between them. An ocean of squandered nature and grinding industry.

Along the street were large, black bags heaving with rubbish, overstuffed bins and broken windows. He would have despaired at the sight, but he'd seen it so many times walking through the district that he felt deadened to it. Only, he did note one thing: The piles were getting bigger with each passing day, but what was one man supposed to do?

The main door to the district was gargantuan, the vehicles meant to pass through it long gone. The metallic edifice, upon closer inspection, was coated in spray paint. Each one an obscene mural of lewd acts and meaningless slogans, epithets and signatures. The sight of it brought a frown to the cleaner's face. Walking up to the side entrance of the upper district, the cleaner quickly presented his identification to the nearby terminal. There was a pause, a dull silence punctuated by a distant car alarm.

A speaker, half covered in graffiti, crackled to life and asked for his name. Blinking at the machine, the cleaner replied, 'Yes. I'm here about the job.'

There came a hurried reply before the speaker shut off and the magnetic lock on the door clicked into place. The cleaner opened the door, a horrible scraping sound stabbing at his ears as it moved along its hinges. Stepping through the threshold, he noted several lamps switch on as he approached. In the newfound light of the lanterns he saw the glimmering surfaces of the complex. A large, golden building – a gaudy monument to the wage-gap and the owner's own self-import.

Around the building itself, past the walls, a sea of dead grass stretched out before him. The water shortage must have struck this place as badly as in the poorer district. Even the rich were losing out. The cleaner gave a smile at the thought.

He walked up to the door, took hold of the bronze knocker in the shape of a long-dead lion, and gave two small wraps against the door. *Thud ... thud*. Letting his hand fall to his side, the cleaner stood in wait. It took a few minutes for the door to be opened. A man the cleaner assumed to be his client opened the door slowly, revealing himself in the light of the hallway beyond. He was a short, beefy man with little in the way of a neck, his face seemed as red as a tomato. The auburn colour of his thinning hair blended with the redness of his skin.

Giving a nervous smile, he spoke: 'Ah, the cleaner. Please, come in.' A hand swept back, gesturing for him to enter the home.

The cleaner processed this, blinking twice and grimacing, 'What's the job?' He walked into the hallway, noting the gold-yellow colouring of the wallpaper, the leaf patterns embossed into the walls. Perhaps they were a remembrance of the long-gone trees, or simply in poor taste.

'You'll see.' The client led the cleaner through the hallway and into the house itself. He continued speaking as they walked, 'It's a simple cleaning job, but I'd prefer that you didn't ask any questions. You're getting paid, of course. Wouldn't expect you to help me for nothing. I'm no cleaner.'

The cleaner scanned the environment, the features that managed to stand out from the warm yellow of the wallpaper. Without looking at the man, he replied, 'Clearly.' The central heating only made the smell worse. A stuffy, cloying stench, the floor strewn with spills and dust. Again, the heat was almost unbearable – a *mocking* heat, the heat of one that could afford such a luxury.

The client let out a small laugh as they casually walked further up and into the complex. They got up to the first floor. He opened the door to what the cleaner surmised was the living room and gestured to go inside. A body lay on the floor, face down, blood pooling around it. A woman, judging by the shape, and the long blonde hair sprawled around their limp head.

The cleaner felt the shock rising in him. *Blood, so much blood ...* His dark eyes widened as he turned to the client: 'What ... did you – '

Before he could continue, the man pulled a wad of cash from his pocket and held it out, 'No questions. I need the floor cleaned. Need *it* cleaned and cleared, too.' He pressed the money into the cleaner's cracked hand and walked out of the room, closing the door behind him.

The cleaner spent what felt like an eternity looking at the door. At length, he turned to face the corpse. He so wished for something more, something sweeter. For the dream he had been promised by the party. No such dream came, and screwing his eyes shut only made the colours swim behind them. The blood thundered in his ears, his fingertips felt cold, severed from the rest of his body.

What do I do? Mind racing, he approached the corpse, making sure to keep clear of the blood. Crouching next to it, he felt his breathing deepen. The wound seemed to be on the front, but he didn't want to turn the body over.

Why did he do this, he thought. *Who were you, what did you do to deserve this?* More thoughts surfaced in his head: *Prostitute, family member, wife, girlfriend ... perhaps just a random woman.* His hand hovered over the corpse's arm.

Don't touch it, he thought, *you have the money, just do your job and leave.* Bolting up with alarming speed, the cleaner began running his hands through his short, brown hair. *Can't just clean – can't just clean it. It's not an animal! Something needs to be ... done.* He remembered the multi-tool, the blade. *If something isn't done, no one will stop him. It will only get worse. Nothing will change. Gap will only get bigger. The selfish will only serve themselves ...*

The cleaner did his job. The blood was mopped up, the body was moved and shoved into a bag. He got his money, the cash burning a hole into his pocket. All the while he grimaced, the image of the woman's corpse sitting behind his eyes. *Coward*, it said to him, *you coward*.

Striding out of the house, he breathed in the choking air, not registering the words of the client as he left. His mind was alight with images of blood, his own screaming guilt rattling around his skull. There were plebeians on the street – not the hyenas, these were grown men, as tired of it all as the cleaner. He watched with vacant eyes as they dumped a few more bags onto the pile before turning to leave.

Through the fog in his brain, the cleaner spoke, 'Wh …' he cleared his throat, 'why are you doing this?'

The man looked confused, 'What? We're putting it here cos it's *rubbish*. Not our fault no one turns up to clear it.'

The cleaner felt his multi-tool in his pocket, remembered the blade yet again. He sighed and hung his head, walking off. The plebeians went about their evening in kind, brushing off the interaction. The cleaner entered his apartment. Sleep alluded him, and so he sat in his chair, looking out of his window at the world.

There was little to see but the grey-brown smog. Little to hear but the shouts of people and the blaring of alarms. The smog filled his brain, poisoning every thought in it. He could not concentrate, could not remember. He was lost, without energy.

The cleaner groaned and placed his head in his hands. He … he was a being of inaction. A cleaner for the people that were killing the world. Even the violence he wished to enact. Everything … it all felt so stifling, pointless.

And so the tears flowed as his world choked itself to death.

Magnus and The Other Place

KATE SQUIRES

'One for you, one for Magnus,' mum says, pushing a coin into my palm and another into the tin on the table. It's a game we've played since I was little. I hold it tight for a moment and make as if I am about to turn, and then smile and give it her back. It's daft really, it's not as if there is anything to buy anyway, but she knows that, it's just a little moment we share. A tradition. Our eyes meet, and I know I see a spark, I mean this could be it. This could be the one. This could change everything. M.A.G.N.U.S.

Mum pulls the cord in tight around her waist and as the material gapes over her chest I glimpse her grubby vest. Mum has strong feelings about food, and it's true we are often hungry, but since we don't really do a lot I guess our needs are less. To be honest no one really eats that much these days. There isn't a lot to choose from and cooking is so expensive. You need pots and pans and a cooker, and power of course. No one wants to be wasting money on silly luxuries now, not when you think of the goodies to come, with Magnus.

Anyway, it's no big deal the hunger – we just carry on and it keeps us all thin after all. Mum says a while back folk were getting obese, eating themselves to death. She said before Magnus people had no dreams or goals so just sat around eating. I worry sometimes as our teeth are often wobbly and our bones are not straight or strong, but we all know that these things are correctable, that when we are with Magnus it will all be fixed. I know this because the people on the pictures near the Magnus machines are all healthy, with bright white teeth and shiny hair. We only really buy tickets now and every penny counts, in the long run being thin will mean less work for the fitness coaches and stylists when our chance comes.

Sometimes in the dark when we lie together all snug, Mum remembers the old days, she tells stories till we fall asleep, about the things I don't remember. I wonder if she really hated it all that much, I mean she talks about it all the time. Still, it breaks up the long nights and takes my mind off my rumbling stomach, and in the end, I always drift off. She talks of a time where people worked day in and day out to earn money only to spend it all on junk and things that really didn't matter. She said people were lonely too, families all separated, spread out all over the place. She said they even put little kids into rooms on their own. Apparently, they used machines to talk to each other and didn't really touch, they just wrote how they felt on screens. Mum says it's good to know how lucky we are, how things have changed for the better since Magnus came.

The benefits are not just around here, when Magnus went international people stopped fighting, there were no more wars. It was as if we were all one big community. Mum said before Magnus, folk were always getting into groups and shouting, blaming each other for all the things wrong with the world. But it's quiet now, Magnus helped restore the peace, we are all in it together and we all want the same thing.

Families are small but close, a ticket is for a household. It's a humble, subtle solidarity, without greed or bragging. We don't really socialise or have friends, there is a general understanding that entertaining is unnecessary. Aside from the unwanted expense, there is also the potential that families could be whisked off to better things at any point, and that friendships would have to be abandoned so it's considered polite to just let folks get on with their lives.

It was a great time to grow up. Bullying and peer pressure were wiped out. We all looked similar, and everyone knew that any little differences could be smoothed out later. Yeah, there were groups of teens who would meet up in the early days, talk about how it was going to be, how Magnus would come, even how we could try and meet up in The Other Place but since everyone had the same goal, and the whole system was random the conversations soon became stale. As the older kids who had memories of fashion and pop music moved on, those of us left didn't have the colours to paint our dreams, so we generally stayed in, and Mum said it was good to rest, especially as the food ran low, to conserve our energy for the future.

Mum and I are together a lot, at home and in the queues. We get on just fine, she likes to talk and I to listen. I am not exactly sure when Dad left, it's one of only the things she doesn't discuss. We missed the coins he used to bring home, but we managed, we had savings. I think we had been spoilt when he was around really, more coins than we needed. He had had one of the few jobs available, servicing the Magnus Machines. No one ever said it but I think him leaving just evened things up a bit. She never voiced it out loud, but I know Mum always hoped he had made it, had been promoted, or snagged a winner. That he would meet us there, at The Other Place. Guess we would just have to wait and see.

When I was younger I half expected him to walk in and take us all away, but I know that's not really how it happens.

No-one ever comes back.

The queues are endless, snaking around the streets, but at least they are calm and quiet. There had been riots at first of course, people pushing and shoving. This had made the authorities sad, they said it had spoiled the gift that it was, left a bad taste in the mouth of Magnus so they had taken away the machines from the areas where people misbehaved, and everyone soon stopped fighting, they just queued longer. Talking in hushed voices, conserving energy. Magnus had lined the streets up to the machines with images of the winners, families holding hands, standing tall on back drops of bright colours. They looked so different from us, I think these pictures helped us focus, reminded us why we did what we did.

It is true that some people just queued. They would shuffle forward until they could purchase that week's allotted tickets and then they would trudge back and rejoin the end, carrying just what they could, I guess they relied upon others doing the same. A simple bartering system helped everyone get what was needed. It was an honest, simple existence. Mum called it purist. I did sometimes wonder, as the pair of us cosied down together at night in our comfort, if maybe we should do the same, that maybe Magnus rewarded those who persevered the hardest.

'Don't worry' Mum said 'The Other Place awaits us all. Magnus really cares.'

The Other Place was set up by the powers of the time to sort out the mess the world had made of itself. We had bled the planet dry, there just wasn't enough to go around, and it was time to fix it. A few important people went first, to pave the way for the rest of us. Pioneers really, trialling the new systems. Who knows what they went through, trying to make a better place for all of us. It was decided that to make the transition easier, a lottery system would be the fairest way of choosing the order in which us ordinary families would join them. That was why Magnus was created. And it really took off, it was marketed so that everyone knew that all the funds raised from the ticket sales, helped increase the capacity of The Other Place, so with every ticket bought your chances of winning improved. As I said, we were all in it together.

Time passed, we queued, and we bought tickets. Every week Magnus was drawn, and people moved on, there wasn't a fuss, they were gone and the rest of us started queuing again. One step nearer the machines, was one step nearer Magnus and the Other Place. Always moving forward, always progressing.

Of course, Mum and I eventually ran out of coins, and things were a little harder. The coins had held all the hope, because without tickets what was there? Panicking, I asked mum what would we do when we had nothing left, and her calmness surprised me. 'Day by day' she would whisper, 'Day by day.' 'Look around,' she said, 'Everyone has something, because everyone is in the queue.' And it's true, there wasn't anyone with nothing. Maybe those who's tickets win, leave their spare coins I thought. We traded what we had in the queues until there was nothing left. Everyone was very supportive, still there is only so much you can do with nothing, and we were resourceful, but there had to be an end.

I am tired now and mum hasn't spoken for days. Her breathing is shallow, and we are both so weak. I could head out, see if I can earn a coin for a ticket but I don't think I can even make it to the queues. I guess I will sit this one out, save my energy. Perhaps tomorrow I will find some food for Mum or a final coin for one last ticket. I go over to Mum and stroke her hair. I tell her stories while she sleeps. In my other hand I hold our very last ticket.

They came in the night. No fanfare, no ceremony or anything. I am not sure how I had imagined it, but it wasn't like this. I woke to movement in our room, big plastic-suited men, torch beams slicing up the dark, they are standing over our bed, I can't make out their faces.

'Who are you? What's happening?' I ask the blackness, trying to sound strong.

'Shh,' said the Magnus man gently. 'Everything is going to be alright.'

The realisation occurs slowly. I try to sit up.

'Is this it? Have we won? Are we going to The Other Place?' He hesitates. Eyes flick to his colleague.

He whispers to me, 'Yes, yes. Congratulations! Shh now, you have won. Everything is going to be alright. You are going to another place, a better place.'

And as I begin to stutter, he leans forward and puts a firm hand on my shoulder.

'Quietly now please, we don't want to upset your neighbours.'

And now I understand, the stealth, the non-event. There is no need for us to be rude, or vain. We are not smug. We are equal. Their turn will come. Magnus is fair. This is right. We deserve this.

I feel so tired. I wish that perhaps I had the energy to savour this moment like I should. To feel anything other than drained. I think of the ticket. They must have checked it while I slept, no-one seems interested in it now. I let it fall. This is it. We have made it. Finally. It was worth it all along, we will meet Dad and ... and to think I nearly gave up, I nearly ...

Wow, it's as if they knew. It's as if they knew how close we came.

I see a man bend and a flash of a silver near my mother's neck, before he scoops her up. Her head lolls back and her arm drops. We are both carried outside to a van, the Magnus man lies me down next to my mother, I see another flash of silver and gasp as the needle pierces my skin. I feel both panic and calm. And I feel really, really tired. I know now that Mum was right. As I close my eyes for the last time, I finally see how much Magnus really cares.

Butterflies

MIA RAYSON REGAN

When you're drowning, there is a point when you give up. Let go and decide that it's over. In a split second your brain tells your lungs to breathe and in that split second, they do. Water rushes down your throat and fills up your lungs so they look like drip bags in the hospital. You suffocate and then you die. When it's cold water though, it's slightly different. Your body can go into shock, and you begin to hyperventilate. Instead of being able to hold your breath for a minute, it can drop to as low as ten seconds. Alas, the same thing happens. Your brain tells your lungs to breathe, and the rush of ice-cold water hurtles down your airways and sinks your lungs like the anchor of a ship. That rush of cold water, that realisation that it is over, and you are just floating instead of fighting, that sinking in your chest; that's what I feel. Every single day.

I parked the car in front of the house and slammed the door as I got out. I pulled my hood up to avoid the rain and ran towards the front door. My fingers were red as I fumbled with my keys trying to get the right one. Something moved in the corner of my eye, and I jumped.

'Frank!' I shrieked. 'You scared me!'

My husband stood staring at a crack in our concrete yard. His hair and shirt were soaked, and he wasn't wearing a coat. I watched him gazing at the floor for a moment. Then I found the key I needed, opened the door and closed it behind me.

I took my coat off and flipped the kettle on. I grabbed two cups from the cabinet and placed a tea bag in each. My therapist has told me to sit in my bath with a cup of tea and let my thoughts float away; like that would resolve anything. After pouring the hot water, mixing milk and adding a heaped teaspoon of sugar, I went back into the rain.

'Frank,' I said through the torrent. 'There's a cup of tea here for you.'

He didn't move. I placed the cup onto the window ledge and watched as the raindrops fell into it. Then I studied him from the warmth of my kitchen and wondered if this is how I'd find him now, every day until he was ready to move on. If he wasn't going to take the next step in this situation, maybe I should.

I got to the top of the staircase and for the first time in weeks, instead of turning left, I turned right. I stood at the door. The letters on it sparkled: 'Ali'. She'd put them up when she was three, sat on Daddy's shoulders to reach. Her room had grown as she had but those letters stayed the same. My fingers traced over each letter. I placed my head against the doorknob, closed my eyes and twisted.

I was instantly hit with the smell of my daughter. The Daisy perfume that she wore every day was engrained in the very walls of the room. The room was the same as it had always been. I looked around at the cream and pink walls with the butterfly stickers flying towards her window. Her bed was made with a pile of pillows and cushions at the headboard. There were no clothes on the floor like there used to be. Her desk was tidy with her eyeshadows stacked neatly in a container to one side, her hair products next to them in a separate box. Her pencil case and notebook in the centre of the desk.

My heart was pounding as I took a step over the

threshold. In the centre of the room, surrounded by her things, it felt so empty. On her bedside cabinet, in a silver frame, was a picture of her and her friends. They'd been on a school trip to the museum. It was really uncool to be excited about a museum, but she'd secretly loved every second of it. She'd always been a history buff like her grandad. I thought she'd pick it as an A level at college. In the picture she smiled the brightest smile. It was the first thing everyone's eyes were drawn to. Becky, her best friend, had jumped on her back as the photo was snapped and the four girls were caught in a flood of giggles. I smiled and hugged the frame, trying to trap the memory.

I sat down on her bed.

'Butterfly bedding?' I asked her.

'Yeah!' she said. 'It's cute!'

'Ali, are you still going to like butterflies when you're eighteen?' I laughed. 'We're not redecorating your room again because you'll be moving out to uni, hopefully.'

'What if I don't want to go to university?' she asked, looking at the little butterflies.

'Well, that's okay too. I want you to do whatever makes you happy, Honey,' I said, stroking her hair.

'Butterflies make me happy,' she said, holding up the bedding.

I laughed and put the bedding in the basket.

The butterflies didn't stop there. They flew onto the stickers on her wall, the notebooks and pencils we bought her for school. Even her clothes started having butterfly patterns on. But three years later, they began to disappear. Her clothes became more solid colours. She favoured red as opposed to pink. She got different notebooks with her monthly allowance. But, like I told her when she picked it, her bedding and her bedroom would keep the butterfly infestation. She must have remembered the conversation though because she never asked to change it. Not once.

I liked to think that her obsession with butterflies as a child was the start of her growing up. She, a butterfly herself, started to change as all children do. When she first grew her wings and wanted her independence, I was more hesitant than Frank. He thought it was time for her to explore the outside world with her friends. I thought it was too soon and was scared that she'd get trapped in a net. I gave her curfews and asked for updates on where she was every few hours.

'Mum,' Ali shouted. 'I'm fine! I'm home, aren't I?'
  'An hour late, Ali! Where were you?'
  'Out with friends like I said,' she argued.
  'Where?' I pressed.
  'We were just on Main Street! Why does it matter?'
  'If you were out shopping why is there mud on your trainers?' I demanded.
  'God, Mum, we live in England! It rains all the time! There's mud in town!' she continued. 'I stepped on a grass patch to let a woman in a wheelchair get past, okay?'
  I glared at her. I saw so much of myself in her. Not just her features but her fiery personality and her kind heart.
  I let out a sigh. 'I'm sorry, Ali. I should trust you.' I pulled her into a hug, and she wrapped her arms around my back. 'I just worry about you that's all.'
  I wiped an escaping tear and kissed her on the head. 'Right, time for bed. I love you.'
  'I love you too,' she said, as I closed her door behind me.

I should have trusted her more when she was being

open with me. It wasn't long after that conversation that she stopped.

'Where's Ali?' I asked Frank one night when I was serving up dinner.

'She said she's not hungry,' he shrugged.

'Well, she needs to eat, Frank,' I said.

'If you can get her off that phone, Erica, be my guest,' he said.

I put the pasta pot down and sighed. 'Serve tea out please,' I said, striding past him.

'Ali!' I shouted at the bottom of the stairs. No answer. 'Ali!' I tried again.

'What?' she finally answered.

'Dinner!' I called back.

'I told Dad, I'm not hungry.'

I ran upstairs and opened her door. Ali was sprawled out across her bed scrolling on Instagram.

'And I'm telling you, you need to eat,' I said, calmly.

'You saying it isn't gonna make me hungry,' she said, without even looking at me.

'Ali!'

'Mum!'

I stormed over to her as she hearted a picture of a woman in a bikini that was much too small for her body.

'Ali! What on earth are you liking?' I grabbed her phone out of her hands and scrolled across the pictures. The skinny woman with big breasts and hips was posing in an array of positions in a tiny matching bikini set. In one of the images, she had her back to a mirror so everyone could see her bum and the side of her boob peeking through the tiny triangle.

'Mum! Give me my phone!' Ali complained.

'This is totally inappropriate, Ali!'

'It's only Kim Kardashian, Mum!' she argued.

'I don't care who it is! She's practically naked!'

Ali just rolled her eyes and said 'You don't understand! She's just advertising her new underwear set!'

'This is underwear?' I gasped.

I could never get hold of her phone again after that. She said that I should stick to my Facebook posts and cat videos. She kept herself in her room scrolling for hours after school.

I should have tried harder to understand her.

I pulled her phone out of the drawer in her bedside cabinet. I plugged it in and waited for it to charge. Eventually the little apple lit the screen up, followed by her lock screen. Her glowing smile drew me in immediately, as it always did. She was hugging Becky and Crystal. The picture was happiness. Taken three weeks before it happened.

'Was Ali depressed?' asked the police officer.

'Not that we know of?' answered Frank. It was a question towards me. 'She'd been keeping to herself lately, but we thought that was what all teenagers do.'

'So, she showed no signs of depression? Self-harm? Suicide?' pressed the officer.

'No nothing like that! Not that I noticed,' said Frank.

'How about you, Mrs Roman?'

I didn't answer. My hands were clasped around the cup of tea that the other police officer had made me.

'Erica?' said Frank, placing a hand on my shoulder.

It broke my trance. 'Sorry, what?'

'How was your relationship with your daughter? Did you notice anything different with her?'

I took a swig of the tea. It didn't help. 'She was quieter. She kept to herself a lot more,' I answered.

'She was always glued to that stupid phone!' said Frank, angrily. He caught my eye and apologised under his breath.

'Can we see the phone please?'

'Why?' I asked.

'We need to take it for evidence,' said the other officer.

'Evidence? Of what?' asked Frank.

'We just need to make sure there's nothing on there that could have harmed Ali.'

The officers left fifteen minutes later with Ali's phone in a plastic bag.

They kept the phone for over a week before returning it.

I turned the rectangle over in my hands. How could such a small thing have caused so much damage? We were a family recovering from a hurricane and this, this little box, was the eye of it.

'We have found evidence that Ali's death was not an act of suicide but rather self-harm,' said a detective.

Frank looked at me.

'You mean,' choked Frank. 'She didn't mean to die?'

'Unfortunately, Mr Roman, Ali did in fact want to take her own life. What I mean is, she was coerced into doing so.'

My eyes snapped up from the cup. Frank stared at me. I stared at the detective, rage building inside me; the first thing I'd felt in a week.

'By whom?' I demanded.

The detective took a deep breath. 'By social media, Mrs Roman.'

'Social media?' I whispered. The rage was surprisingly gone as quickly as it had appeared.

'Yes,' he continued. 'It appears that in Ali's last few weeks of life, she had researched depression and suicide on multiple social media platforms. Some of the things she saw almost ...' he paused.

'Go on,' I said.

'Some of the content glorified suicide and self-harm and normalised depression,' the detective hesitated. 'Some posts included different ways in which to tie a rope to hang yourself.'

'Oh my god,' gasped Frank, slapping his hand across his mouth. He leaned himself into my chest and began to sob.

'Could we have stopped it?' I asked.

'You mustn't blame yourselves.'

When he recovered, Frank asked to see what our daughter had seen. The detective protested but Frank said he needed to see what evil had tormented his little girl. He didn't sleep for a week afterwards. It came out later in a report, that some of the content Ali had seen had been brought to her attention by an algorithm. She hadn't even searched it herself.

I unplugged the phone and threw it back in the drawer. I fell back on her bed and cuddled her small bear that was propped up against the pillows.

Finally, I began to cry. Tears streamed down my face and mixed into the teddy and my hair. I cried so hard it hurt to breathe. Teardrops fell onto the little pink butterflies. I curled into a ball and let myself grieve.

Some time later, I don't know how long, I finally stopped. I placed Ali's bear back in its spot on her bed. I straightened out the crinkles that I'd created in the bedding and walked to the door. I looked back at her room.

'I love it!' she gasped when she first walked in, after we'd finished decorating. 'It's exactly what I wanted.'

We smiled back at her. It'd taken us all weekend, but her butterfly bedroom was finished.

'Thank you!' said Ali.

'You're welcome, Baby,' I whispered and closed the door to the empty room.

I ran myself a bath. I sprinkled some of the butterfly bath floats that I'd gotten her for Christmas. Even though she'd grown out of her butterfly phase, I still bought her something with them on every year. They floated along the water as I stepped in. I laid down and with a final breath, I let myself sink as the colours bled into one.

Mothers

MICHAEL HARGREAVES

She hadn't eaten in four days, except the rat. She'd boiled its bones in a pot of rainwater and slurped it like broth. She kept the organs she couldn't eat as bait. Her Dad taught her how to cook, and how to catch animals. There'd been more the past few years, but they were harder to catch now. They seemed smarter than when Dad showed her. With rats, he taught her to play dead and wait for them to come. It can take hours or days, but you don't burn much energy and it's the only way to get close enough. With cats and dogs, he taught her other ways. She wiped her bloody hands on her trousers.

You have to get back now, Dad's voice echoed like a ghost in her mind, *you need to cook it and take care of that leg.*

She could have plunged her hands inside the bloody knife wound in the dog's side. Tore it apart. Eaten it raw. Her stomach churned and the sides of her jaw tingled, begging her to do it.

You'll get sick, Dad reminded her, *Move.*

She grunted as she staggered to her feet. Sharp pains burned as blood trickled from the teeth marks in her shin. The trap was rusty, so it took her a few tries to open it and free the dog. She shuffled her long ruck sack around it and then lifted it up and shook the dog inside like she was changing a pillow. The other dogs cried in the distance. They had snarled and barked and snapped their teeth at her, and each time she batted them away with a hammer and knife. One of them was bleeding from where she'd stabbed it. The same one that bit her shin. Now that the dog in the trap was dead and silent, they kept their distance, pacing across some invisible threshold and whimpering mournfully. She stared at them, remembering the flickering fire at her Mum's feet as Dad carried her away into the blackness. Flames rose through her throat.

They'd do the same to you, Dad snapped.

You don't know that, Mum whispered in reply.

She shook off the nausea and winced as she picked up the back. It was too heavy, and her leg hurt too much. She froze, eyes wide, heart tingling. The dogs yapped and sprinted down the road. The sound. Sputtering. Popping. Rumbling. An engine. They were coming.

Run! Dad urged.

Hide, Mum corrected. *You can't run with your leg.*

She scanned the area desperately. Houses with broken windows and bombed-out holes in the roofs.

They'll check the houses first, Mum warned.

Move now! Dad continued

There were garden walls covered in brown, dusty weeds.

They'll see over them.

They're coming!

Muffled voices hummed in the distance under the rumbling of the engine.

She shuffled under the burnt-out shell of an abandoned car. She reached forward and dragged the bag with her. She placed her hand over her mouth and took deep breaths to steady herself.

They're here, Mum and Dad gasped.

An old scrap collecting truck appeared around the corner. It stuttered forward and coughed smoke from the exhaust. Two men sat in the front and two walked alongside. Machetes swung from their hands. The cage on the back of the truck rattled with the engine. It was crammed with people. Naked. Shivering. The sharp ridges of their ribs and hips bulged under their thin, tight skin. It was as if their bones could break through at any moment. Some clasped their bloody fingers in the links in the cage roof, clambering over others to get room and air. Others clutched children in the corner, shielding them and pushing back against the fidgeting weight of those fighting for space. A few were flopped on the floor, with flies sucking the glistening dew from their wide, still eyes.

The truck hissed and popped and grinded to a stop a few feet from her.

'Shit!' One of the men in the truck said as he got out. He was tall and gangly and had a long stringy beard. 'It needs a new cooler.'

'We'll trade one of these,' a shorter man wacked the cage with his machete.

The people in the cage flinched and cried. The tall man opened the bonnet. Steam sizzled up as he looked inside.

The woman watched as a huge pair of boots thumped the concrete just in front of her face. A wrinkly man kneeled down next to the bloody trap and ran his fingers across it.

'Someone's been through here,' he called and looked around. 'Check the houses.'

You idiot! Dad growled. *I told you to run!*

She would have been caught, Mum snapped back.

She's about to be ...

Two of the men marched into the house across the street.

'I'll check the cars.' Another man said. 'You get it started again.' He instructed.

She gasped and her heart sped as the man's boots thumped the concrete and stormed towards her.

Remember what we talked about, Dad said.

No! Mum begged.

She clutched the knife in her pocket. The man knelt by the car and fiddled with the fuel cap and fed a rubber pipe inside and sucked through the other end. He coughed and caught his breath, his dirty fingers crept down, inches from her face, and scratched his leg. She gripped the knife tighter.

The two men climbed back out of the window.

'Nothing,' one called. 'Anything under the cars?'

The words rang through her like a fire alarm. This was it. She pressed the knife into her throat and closed her eyes.

It's okay, Dad said. *Just like we talked about.*

The man who was kneeling next to the car grunted with pain as he shuffled his legs around.

Something will happen, Mum cried. *Just wait!*

It's already happening, Dad said, calmly.

She grimaced as a tear trickled down her cheek. She slashed at the air, panting and tensing her mouth to muffle her whimpers. Dad had explained it so simply. So coldly. The same way he talked about building a fire or taking care of your feet. But it was hard. She didn't think she was afraid to die, but now that it was here, she thought of all the death she'd seen. Caused. Everything struggled. Everything fought. Everything ran. And now so was she.

Don't mess this up! Dad shouted. *Think about what they'll do when they find you.*

The man planted his hand on the ground and growled uncomfortably as he dipped down.

If they find you, Mum corrected.

'You idiot!' one of the men working on the truck screamed at the other, shoving him to the ground. 'You're breaking it!'

The other man sprung up and launched himself forward. They collapsed to the ground and wrestled and punched and bit each other.

'For fuck's sake!' The man coughed as he stood up and walked over to the front of the truck to separate the men.

She noticed the short gap between her car and theirs. It was clear. She left the dog, crawled across the concrete and shuffled under the truck. Her heart drummed as she lay flat on her stomach and listened. The men shouted at each other before one cut in.

'That's enough!' he ordered. 'Just get it running!' He walked past the side of the car and kneeled down. 'Look at this!' He dragged the bag from under the car and opened it. 'They must have run when they heard us.'

The truck engine coughed above her and struggled to start.

Now what, Dad said, almost gloatingly.

Maybe they won't see you when they drive off, Mum rebuffed.

Some of them are walking. And even if they don't, the people in the cage will call for help, Dad sighed.

She swivelled her head, desperate for an escape. A plan. Someway she could creep away without being noticed. It was too open, and the men weren't distracted anymore. The engine sputtered and choked. They'd drive over her and she'd be on show for them. She pressed the knife to her throat again.

No mistakes this time, Dad insisted.

She closed her eyes and her wrist trembled as she pressed the knife on her skin. The engine chugged and rumbled steadily.

Just wait! Mum screamed.

'Let's go,' one of them called over the engine and rattling cage.

Her eyes popped open.

She put the knife in her pocket and crawled on her front to the back of the car before spinning around and pulling herself up on the bumper. She reached up and grabbed the L-shaped bolt on the bottom of the cage door and twisted and pulled and grabbed it with both hands and hung off it with all her weight. Her elbows slammed into the concrete as it came loose. She shuffled back under the truck as the cage doors flung open. Pairs of bare feet slapped the road as all the people clambered out of the cage and sprinted away. Men. Women. Children.

'Shit!' one of the men called before running after them. 'Turn it around!' he called.

The truck moved forward and turned. The back wheel rolled towards her groin.

Grab something! Dad shouted.

She reached up and gripped a pipe under the car and picked her feet up, panting and fighting back panicked whimpers. The truck dragged her along the concrete. Forward. Her lower back burned on the ground. Backwards. Her grip slipped and her shoulder blades clattered against the concrete. Forward. Black.

Eva watched the embers from the fire rise into the black air. Her Mum wrapped her arms around her from behind and hugged her blanket tighter over her chest and shoulders. Dad appeared under the bridge and dropped a heap of sticks and twigs next to the dwindling fire. He poked it and got it going again. Eva squelched into the wet ground with her boots and giggled at the sound. Dad sat down across the fire and glanced side to side nervously before pulling out a small chunk of moss.

'I think it's safe,' he said as he nibbled the corner. They'd have to wait a few hours before they could share the rest. 'There are some people on the other side of the village,' he said to Mum.

'Good people?' she chirped.

'There are no good people,' he muttered.

'Except us,' she replied. 'We'll leave in the morning,' she rubbed Eva's shoulders.

'Where will we go?' Dad stared into the fire with a dead expression.

'Somewhere,' she said calmly.

Dad's eyes snapped up to her from the fire. He moved around and kneeled next to Eva and covered her ears with his filthy hands. She could still hear.

'It's not too late,' he whispered. 'We won't make it two days before we starve. Or they catch us.'

'They won't catch us,' she argued.

'How do you know?'

'I don't.'

They sat in silence for a moment. Dad tutted and shook his head. The tears in his eyes glinted with the fire.

'You know what they'll do if they catch you both,' he whispered again. 'Every week, you say it'll get better. That we'll find food. Shelter. Good people to protect us. And every week, it gets worse. Everything gets more dead. There's no food. Nowhere safe. No good people.'

'We're good people,' she said.

Dad's eyes flashed wide, and he sprung up and ran outside the bridge and stood there listening.

'We have to go!' he growled, running back and stuffing what he could into his backpack.

Mum took her hands off Eva's ears. Voices echoed in the night air over the crackling fire. Mum took the blanket and gave it to Dad to put in the bag. He dug his fingers into the wet ground and tossed heaps onto the fire to put it out. It steamed and hissed. He grabbed Mum's hand.

'Come on!' he pulled. 'They're too close!'

Mum snatched her arm back. Dad frowned and tried again, but she wrestled her arm away.

'What are you doing?' he mumbled.

'The fire.'

'I've put it out,' he hurried, 'Let's go.'

'It's hot.' she shrugged.

'So what?'

'They'll expect someone here.'

Dad's mouth opened. The voices were louder. There were several men. The flames from their torches cackled in the night. He shook his head.

'Stop it!' he grunted. 'We have to go.'

'*You* have to go,' Mum resisted again. 'You can get her further faster.'

Dad went to speak, but Mum shoved her hand around his mouth. 'There's no time. I'll see you soon, okay?'

He paused and locked eyes with her. He snatched Eva up into his chest. She wrapped her legs and arms around him like she'd done a hundred times before.

'Mum?' she whimpered.

'I'll see you soon, Eva,' she kissed her head and nodded to Dad, who turned and ran off into the black woods.

The thin branches from dead trees whipped his face as he scrambled through the dark. She clung on and cried and squawked.

'Shut up!' he rasped, as he ran down a hill into a clearing. A bright flame erupted from the blackness ahead of them. A young man held a torch and pointed a gun at them. Dad froze in the orange glow of the flaming torch. The young man's lip was trembling. Ash and embers shook off the torch, dancing in his wet, blue eyes.

'P-Please …' Dad sobbed. 'Y-You don't h-have to …'

She could feel his heartbeat as she cried and clutched

him tightly. The young man's teeth chattered, and he panted. He put his finger on the trigger. The gun rattled in his quivering hand. A shriek filled the air from the blackness behind Dad. She knew it was her mum. Dad exhaled and swallowed as he crossed his arms around Eva's neck. He held his breath and started squeezing. She coughed for air and slapped his back and uncrossed her legs and swung them desperately. He squeezed and squeezed. He knew this was better. He knew what they might do if they took her. Twinkling specs of light filled her vision. The young man lowered the gun and the torch.

'That way,' he whimpered, pointing the torch to the right.

Dad relaxed his arms and Eva gasped for air.

It was dusk when Eva woke up. Her head burned and stung as she peeled her face from the cold concrete. She rubbed her scalp and flakes of dried blood snowed down. There was a pool of dried blood where she'd rested. She remembered the truck and the men and staggered to her feet in a panic. Her leg burned as she put weight on it. She looked around. Melted cars. Burned houses. The bag. She was alone.

You were knocked out by the bumper, Dad said.

Eva limped towards the bag and grunted as she heaved it up and hooked the strap over her shoulder. She struggled down the street and made her way back to the chapel she'd made her home. She knew the way, even in the darkening night. She weaved between the holes in the concrete. It took her half an hour to get a mile down the road, where the chapel was. The windows had been smashed and there was an attached building that was black and charred. The main tower, with the vestry and the altar, hadn't been burned, but it'd been raided long before she arrived and there was nothing valuable there. She liked it because she could see a long way from the top. She grimaced and growled as she powered up the stairs. She grunted through gritted teeth and spat with effort. She reached the top, dropped the bag and collapsed to her knees.

Keep going, Mum said.

She shook her head and grabbed the door handle to help herself up. Blood. It was black in the dark, and it was still wet.

Someone's inside, Dad said, *but they're injured.*

She took out the knife and steadied herself. She needed the fire to cook the dog. And everything for the fire was inside. She nudged the door open and peaked inside. There was a woman in rags lying on the altar. She was bleeding from her stomach. The door creaked open as Eva stepped through and looked around for anyone else. Once she knew it was clear, she dragged the dog inside and shut the door and limped over holding the knife forward.

'You need to leave!' Eva shouted.

The woman groaned and tried to sit up. Her face was grey and her lips were cracked and pale. 'Please.' She managed.

Don't listen to her, Dad said.

'Get out!' Eva screamed.

'I can't …' The woman coughed.

Eva looked down at the woman. Her thin rags were soaked with cold blood and there was a deep gash in her side.

'You're dying,' Eva lowered the knife.

The woman chuckled, 'No shit,' she dragged herself along the floor and shouted in pain as she propped herself up against the rotten organ.

A high-pitched scream echoed through the chapel. Eva

turned. A young boy sprinted towards her and swung a stick at her. She stepped back and it missed. She pinned the boy to the ground and put the knife to his throat. He glared up at her through his sky-blue eyes.

'He's scared!' the woman croaked. 'Please!'

Eva snarled at the boy and turned to the woman. 'You both need to leave,' she let the boy go and got to her feet.

'Please …' she cried. 'Help us.'

The boy crawled over to her and hugged her.

They're not your problem. Dad said. *Someone will be looking for them.*

And you found them … Mum replied. *The woman doesn't have long.*

'You can die here,' Eva whispered. 'The boy can take you when you do.'

She limped back through the vestry and grabbed the bag and brought it back to the broken window above the fire pit and set it going with an old flint and some Bible pages. There weren't many pages left. But they were thin and caught fire fast and strong. She took the dog out and tended to the fire while she carved at it and pulled apart the flesh and organs and skewered them.

'How old are you?' the woman asked.

Eva didn't reply. The boy whimpered on his mother.

'You can't have seen twenty winters,' The woman continued. 'How have you survived this long on your own?'

'I don't know how old I am,' Eva snapped. 'My dad taught me.'

'Smart man,' she grunted in pain. 'And your mother?'

'She died,' Eva muttered.

'Maybe I'll see her soon,' The woman said. 'I could tell her how you helped us.'

She's trying to trick you, Dad bleated.

'No talking,' Eva said as she rotated the liver of the dog over the flames. It hissed and popped as the liquids inside steamed. Eva bit her lip. She hadn't spoken to anyone in years. Since Dad. She didn't know when she would be able to again. 'Where did you come from?'

'East,' She began. 'We were caught just outside of the town – they put us in a cage. They said they were farmers. I know what that means.'

'Me too,' Eva chipped in. 'It means they sell people to other people. Make them have babies and sell them too.'

'It was a miracle we escaped,' The woman said. 'We stopped about a mile from here. And the cage door just opened. We poured out and ran, but one caught us. I managed to get him off us, but he did this.' She gestured to her bleeding side.

Eva realised that she recognised the rags. She'd freed them without knowing, and now they were here.

'There are no miracles,' Eva said as she snatched the skewer, turned away from the woman and boy, and sank her teeth into the black liver. She moaned as she swallowed and let it fill her stomach.

'Mummy?' The boy said. There was no reply. 'Mummy!?' He screamed again and again, crying and spitting all over her.

Eva shook her head and tensed her jaw. *You can't leave the boy*, Mum said. *Yes, you can.* Dad insisted. Eva looked into the open husk of the dog and noticed something. She frowned and dug her hands around a small sack at the bottom of the abdomen. She'd never seen that before in an animal. And she'd eaten dogs before. She took out the knife and cut into the slimy pouch. A clear liquid squirted out and she reached in. It was soft and had a strange shape to it. It wasn't like any organ she'd seen before. Her face fell vacant. Its tiny limbs. Its flat, featureless face. Its pink skin. Eva dropped the foetus and coughed herself into tears. She turned her back to the woman and boy and did her best not to make any noise. But she sniffled. The boy's cries were louder and hers went unnoticed.

I didn't mean to, she swore to her mum.

I know, she replied. *But you didn't mean not to, either.*

Eva waited, expecting her mum to say something else. Something comforting. Something hopeful. But there was nothing. She looked over at the boy, whose face was buried in his mother's chest. The woman's face was slack and her eyes were wide. Eva sat for a moment. Her eyes moved between the cooked dog liver and the foetus and the boy.

Don't ... Dad whispered.

Eva picked up the liver and limped over to the boy. She poked him and he flinched and cowered from her. Her face felt strange as she forced a smile. The boy's lower lip quivered as she offered him the liver.

The Great North Plain

DOMINIC RIVRON

1st June

Last night I had a dream about the Great North Plain. What exactly happened in it I've no idea. All that remained of it, on waking, was a feeling that I'd been there a moment before, stood on the edge of the forest, looking out over that red, rocky expanse. The feeling played on my mind all morning. By lunchtime, I'd decided to drive up and visit the place. I hadn't been there for a while and it would be a pleasant thing to do on a warm, summer afternoon.

It's sheep-farming country round here. Rounded hills just bleak enough to be good for nothing else. The hills go on for miles but if you keep driving north, all of a sudden, the fields full of sheep give way to a dense pine forest. The road is so straight you just know it was built by the Romans. Up and down the hills it goes, first the fields then dense rows of pine trees on either side, until it comes to an abrupt end. It's just as if the road-builders ran out of tarmac.

This is where the plain begins. Beyond this point, there are no trees, no grass, no hills. An expanse of red rock as flat as the ocean stretches away as far as the eye can see. Pictures convey nothing of the awe you feel when you stand on the edge of it. I say it's flat but when seen close, the surface is rough and broken – anyone trying to walk over it would make slow progress. If you ever make the journey up north to see it for yourself, you'll find a number of cars parked up on the verges where the road comes to an end. A few of them have been there for a while, left by people who set off to explore. On some, the tyres and windscreen-wipers have perished and a film of dirt clouds the windows. A lot of those who venture out onto the plain never return. If you search the internet you'll find there are many theories for this. The surface is so featureless you can quickly lose your bearings. Deposits of magnetic rock cause compasses to malfunction. It's also said to be difficult to get a mobile phone signal from there, although no-one seems able to explain why. Heat rising from the rock, it's said, can cause the formation of mirages, causing images to form in the air close to the horizon. People might see, say, an image of the forest edge and make for it, thinking they're retracing their steps to the road, when in fact they're walking deeper into the plain. There are said to be deep shafts between the rocks in places, often surrounded by scree and all too easy to slip into. There are even stranger theories, too, of discontinuities in space and time. Then there are stories of animals that have strayed onto the plain being found there dead and inexplicably mutilated. Scientists send drones out over it to map it and gather data but often the data is sent back corrupted or the drones disappear. An added complication is that geological time on the plain seems to pass more quickly than it does everywhere else. The features of a given area can change beyond recognition in the course of a few years, or even a few months.

Driving up through the forest, I found myself thinking about my friend Michael and the hill-walking expeditions we'd been on together. The straightness of the road and the pine trees reminded me of one such in particular, though I could remember very little else about it. The curious, fragmentary nature of the memory had me wondering if it was a memory at all, or just part of another dream I'd had. But no, it was far too vivid to be a dream. The more I thought about it, the more I could remember of the actual conversation we'd had – about how the road was so straight, it had to be a Roman road – only my memory of the conversation came to an abrupt end, just like the road itself. I felt sure we'd gone on to climb a hill, as we always did. Only, where that hill might be, I'd no idea. I could remember nothing whatsoever about it.

It was the middle of the week. Had it been the weekend or the school holidays, the place would've been packed with sight-seers. A burger-van would be parked up in the rutted lay-by close to the road-end. As it was, I had the place to myself. I parked up and made my way on foot to the point where the crumbling tarmac topped the short drop of loose earth and stones that sloped down to the edge of the expanse of red rock.

I had no desire to clamber down and venture out onto the plain, even for a short distance. The older I get, the more risk-averse I get. (When Michael and I go off walking together these days, I like the hills we climb to be grassy, not rocky, and not too steep.) I was quite happy to stay where I was, safe by the road, on the grass under the trees, at the edge of the forest. I could appreciate the curious geography of the plain with its rough plates of rock, it fissures and its scree-funnels, from where I stood. I could feel that sense of wonder any massive natural phenomenon tends to invoke. This, I felt sure, was exactly where I'd been standing in my dream. Standing there brought on no dramatic revelation, though: whatever had taken place in my dream remained intractably forgotten. It came as no surprise. I lit up a cigarette. The click of the lighter sounded curiously loud. People often talk about the silence of the plain and how it's almost as imposing as the sight of it. As the composer John Cage once said, *silence is a real sound*. He might've been thinking of the plain when he said it. The silent sound it makes is like a void that stretches to the horizon. You can almost reach out and touch it. The more you listen though, the more you hear: the grating of a distant rock as it shifts an inch or two. A trickle of displaced scree. Occasionally you might hear the cry of a bird, although it's said that birds tend to avoid flying over the plain. If the surface of the plain – as has often been said – is like that of another planet, the almost tangible silence that lays over it could almost be its atmosphere.

Where had we been going, Michael and I? I'd have to ask him, see if he could remember. I decided to drop by on my way back, if he was in. It wouldn't take me far out of my way. I took out my phone and dropped him a text. He replied in less than a minute. *See you soon!*

I followed Michael through to the living room and sat myself down. Unlike me, he's a fastidious man. Also, unlike me, he lives alone. The attraction of opposites, perhaps. There were daffodils in a vase on the windowsill and the room bore a faint scent of the flowers. He made us both a pot of tea. We fell to talking about our past escapades in the hills. I asked him about the Roman road and the pine forest.

'Are you thinking of Black Pike?' he said.

I told him I didn't think I was. We'd climbed Black Pike quite a few times.

'Maybe not. But the mind can play tricks,' he said, getting up and reaching down an Ordnance Survey map. He opened it out on the coffee table. An irregular area that ran across the whole top of the sheet was conspicuously blank: The Great North Plain. He ran his finger down, past where we lived, to Black Pike. 'I mean, look, these woods –' He pointed to the place on the map where the road we usually took to get to the pike ran through a wood. I shook my head.

'But the road winds and the trees are deciduous,' I said. 'I'm sure that's not the place I was thinking of. The road I'm thinking of was straight. There were pine trees either side, just like the road up to the plain.'

Michael shrugged. 'As I said, the mind plays tricks,' he said.

'We talked about it being a Roman road, I'm sure,' I said.

'We've driven up to the plain together more than once. Perhaps it was then. Perhaps you're conflating the two: Black Pike and the Great North Plain.'

'Maybe,' I said. But I wasn't convinced.

'Whatever,' he said. 'We should go for another walk together again, soon, though. It's been a while.'

I concurred.

I left Michael's with an uncanny feeling: my mind may well have been playing tricks on me, but I couldn't escape the fact that it felt more as if it were reality that was playing the tricks. It was this feeling that led me to write down all the above. If I didn't, it would be all too easy to dismiss it as an aberration.

26th June

Today I came across the spiral-bound notebook in which I'd written my notes of the 1st June. For the next few days I'd had a whole lot of routine jobs to sort out. The whole business of the plain was pushed out of my mind. I'd encountered no more disturbing anomalies, had no reason to think the world I was living in was any different to that experienced by those around me. If, as time went on, my thoughts ever turned to the business of the plain, I'd dismissed it as 'one of those things', as people say, and moved on. Re-reading these notes though, the circumstances that led me to write them seemed, to my surprise, no less uncanny to me than they had at the time. I didn't know what to think. I was interested to see what my house-mate, Alison, thought about it all. I found her in her studio, the upstairs back room of the house. She'd chosen it because of the light. It has two big windows and faces south. She manages to bring in a steady income selling landscapes to the tourists. There was one half-finished on the easel as I came in. She was sitting close by it, smoking a cigarette. I read her what I'd written.

'The forest is a nice touch,' she said.

'How do you mean?' I said.

'The way you made up the forest. I mean, there isn't a forest on the road to the north. It's a while since I've been there, but I'm sure the hills just come to an end at the plain.'

'There is,' I said. 'I was there. There again, there's more than one road up there. There are side-roads. Perhaps we're thinking of different roads.'

She thought for a moment. 'I still can't think of any forests up that way. It doesn't matter though. It adds to the effect. I mean, look ...' She pointed with her brush to the foreground of the picture she was working on. 'There isn't a rock there in real life. I put it in while I was sketching because it looked right. It balances up the composition.'

Back downstairs, I took out my Ordnance Survey map to check. The top third, of course, the Great North Plain, was completely blank. Not so much as a contour line. Below it lay an area of roads, hills and villages. No sign of a forest. If the map were to be believed, Alison was right. Perhaps mine was an old map? A commercial pine forest can grow to a respectable height in twenty years. Perhaps the last time Alison was there there were no trees. It sounded unlikely (I felt sure the trees I'd driven through were older than that), but it was enough to convince me there could be a rational explanation, if only I knew what it was. I was left with the same uncanny feeling I'd felt after my visit to Michael's place. I went back to my notebook and brought my notes up to date.

30*th* June

Michael rang. He said we needed to get round to organising the walk we'd talked about at our last meeting. We fixed a date and agreed we'd decide where to go nearer the time. We got talking about other things. He asked after Alison. I started to tell him about the conversation I'd had with her, but he soon picked me up on something I said.

'The Great *North* Plain?' he said. 'You know, you're the only person I know who calls it that. It stretches away to the west, too, and even extends into the south.'

I said perhaps I'd slipped into calling it that because we lived close to its northern edge. To be honest, though, I was intrigued. On my visits, I'd only ever stood at the end of the road and looked out over the plain to the northern horizon. It struck me how I'd never given much thought to how far it extended to the west – or to the east, for that matter. I took down a map of the western region and spread it out. Sure enough, the left-hand side of the sheet was completely blank. I then took down the map of the southern region. The left side of this wasn't blank but a long peninsula of nothingness extended down from the top of it, dwindling to a point in the lower third of the map. My geography might not be great, but there was no getting away from the fact: the plain was spreading. Somehow roads, hills, forests and villages – not to mention towns, cities, railway lines and everything else – were silently disappearing. Not only that but, somehow, people seemed to be losing their memories of the things that had disappeared. There'd been nothing about it on the news, either. It all made no sense. Thinking all this through, I felt a cold wave pass over me. I lit up a cigarette to calm my nerves. It got worse. Even if I could convince the world of what was happening, what could be done about it? I'm no scientist, but it seems as if reality is changing in ways outside our experience and beyond our comprehension. I took out my notebook and brought my account up-to-date again. I wish I could, and I'll have to give it some thought, but I can think of nothing else I can do for now. And I have to face the fact that perhaps it's all in my head: perhaps I'm going mad. If I am, then at least I'll be able to refer back to what I've written. If I need to see a doctor it might help them diagnose what the problem is.

1st July

I found Alison working on her latest landscape, a group of sheep sheltering from a storm behind a drystone wall. (As is usual with Alison, the sheep had an anthropomorphic look about them. Their faces were well-painted, accurate sheep-faces, but the expressions on them were uncannily human. They looked like people facing discomfort with stoicism. Her dealer reckoned it was the faces on her sheep that sold her pictures). I told her I'd been talking to Michael again. I asked her what she knew about the extent of the plain. Given my conversation with Michael, and the latest evidence of the maps, I was curious to know what she'd say.

'I don't know,' she said. 'Is this a quiz or something?' She sounded slightly annoyed. 'I never was any good at Geography at school. I know we live on a peninsula of fertile land that extends into it. It connects us to the cities in the south. Don't tell me,' she added, 'you're going to write down everything I just said. Sometimes I worry about you.' She jabbed at the canvas with her paintbrush a little more fiercely than usual.

8th July

This morning I ran out of cigarettes. I went looking for Alison to see if I could cadge a couple to see me through. I went up to her studio. She wasn't there. She'd left her cigarettes and lighter, though, on the table beside her easel. As I reached down for them, I couldn't help but notice the painting stood on it. It wasn't one of her 'tourist sheepscapes' as she called them in her more cynical moments. The upper half was a dramatic, sunset sky, the lower half an expanse of broken, red rock, stretching away into the distance. It was the plain. Quite how, I don't know, but somehow she'd captured – brilliantly, I thought – the ambiguities of its geography, the mirage-like uncertainty of the horizon and even the palpable strangeness of its atmosphere. It drew you in. Stood there before it, I could even hear the silence. What was it? *Silence is a real sound.* I took out one of her cigarettes and lit it. The click of the lighter sounded curiously loud. Momentarily distracted, I looked up from the easel to the window. I knew what I was going to see there before I saw it: nothing but the sky and an expanse of broken, red rock, stretching away into the distance.

Finding the Door

WILLIAM THIRSK-GASKILL

I am a patient with dementia in Saint James's Hospital in Leeds, England. I don't know what year it is where you are. The virtual reality environment through which this is being mediated has its own calendar, which is currently in the year 1049. To you, that may connote swords or Edward the Confessor. To me, it is a whim of the system administrators, and just something I have to live with.

One of the things I am grateful for about the virtualisation of my life is that I did not have to do it myself, but the people who undertook it did a good, thorough job. I have a library in my virtual apartment, with shelves containing all the albums of photographs from my life. I always know where they are. They never get dusty or dirty, or accidentally wiped off an electronic device, and my enjoyment of them is protected against fire, unless the fire were to happen in the hospital ward where my body is, in which case I would not need to worry about photographs.

My conscious mind has almost no useful function left at all. If I were brought back to full consciousness, and you gave me something like a TV remote control, not only would I probably lose it and have no recollection of where I had left it, but I would not be able to remember what it was for. My last memories of the actual world are fleeting glimpses of the period during which I became severely symptomatic. I underwent detailed assessment, and it was found that the tissue that supported my subconscious mind was still sound, and would, as far as anybody could tell, remain so for a long time.

I am kept permanently asleep by drug therapy, but my subconscious mind is constantly fed with data. Because my subconscious mind is functioning, I need to maintain a metabolic rate which is at least 30 percent of normal, and so I need nutrients. These are fed to me intravenously, and the end product metabolites eliminated by dialysis. My stomach and intestines have been removed. I won't be needing them again. I get my enjoyment of eating and drinking through the virtual reality experience. My body can breathe unassisted, but my respiration is monitored, and I would be given oxygen if I were to go into respiratory distress.

The data bridge to my subconscious mind is a two-way link. I can send messages, as well as receive them.

This environment has all the vices of the actual world available to those who want them, but recreational drugs, including alcohol, are not what they are in the actual world. Drinking virtual alcohol does make your vision blurred and walking more difficult, but that is about all, and it is not much fun.

Despite the fact that my body is asleep, and will remain so for the rest of my actual life, I have a job, and a certain amount of correspondence to deal with. All communication is mediated through the virtual reality environment, via the data bridge. The virtual city I live in is a fictionalised version of Los Angeles in the 1940s, and so my messages arrive either in the mail, or over the phone. I don't have a phone in my apartment, but I do have one in my office. My business letters are also delivered to the office. I also have a cheat device. It looks like a pocket watch, but it can send text, and every message it sends to the Client Egress Sub-division is automatically assigned top priority.

Some of my business letters are about my tenancy in this virtual environment. Some of the rent is paid for by actual social services, and the rest from my actual estate. Ninety percent of my pension goes towards paying for my tenancy. The other 10 percent appears as dollars in the virtual environment. That does not amount to very much, which is one reason why I have a virtual job. It keeps me occupied. I find it fulfilling, and I am good at it, but I know that I am paying for my own end of life care, at the point of delivery. My body and my conscious mind have retired, but my subconscious mind will only get to retire when I die. The corporation which hosts the virtual environment is called Cygnet Healthcare.

People who live permanently in virtual reality do not have the right to vote in actual elections, even though the technology to enable us to do so is readily available.

If my rent is not kept up to date, I can be evicted from the virtual environment. If the eviction process went to completion, which would usually take about three months of actual time, my nutrient feeds would be withdrawn, and I would die.

I am sitting in my office chair, going through the intray. I deal with anything that looks official first, particularly if it has a Cygnet Healthcare frank on it. This letter from Cygnet is about a change to my care plan. I have decided to take up the offer of a discount on a new screening programme, in return for my body being moved to an out-of-town facility where the physical rent is lower. The screening programme is mainly to check for cancer, and includes a full body MRI scan every six months. MRI scans are much less nerve-wracking if your body is in a state of chemically-induced coma while it is happening. The letter confirms that my body will be moved tomorrow, on January 27, 1049. All dates and times are according to the standard that this environment uses. The speed that this environment runs at is supposed to be the same as actual reality, not that this matters. No action from me is required. The letter assures me that I should not notice anything, and to let Cygnet know if there is any variation in the service. Such events are very rare, but are not unknown. A patch was incorrectly installed last year, which affected the resolution of the graphics, and made everything look like a video game from the early 1980s, but it was soon fixed. Everybody affected got a month's rent reimbursed.

After I have finished reading the letter from Cygnet, I go through the correspondence for my own business. The lettering on my office door says, William Hopper, Private Investigator. William Hopper is an anagram of Philip Marlowe. The name William Hopper has some reputation in this environment. I am on the right side of most of the local law enforcement officers, and can sometimes pull strings, if I have to. 'Local law enforcement officers' is my vernacular expression for the technical departments of Cygnet Healthcare, chiefly the Client Egress Sub-division.

The next letter I open looks like this:

Mrs Josephine Teesdale
251 Paradise Mansions
Beverley Hills
Los Angeles
CA #27054

January 25, 1049

Mr William Hopper
Room 117
Providential House
1109 Lincoln Avenue
Los Angeles
CA #25325

Dear Mr Hopper,

Your name was given to me by the daughter of my dear sister, Georgina (Hernandez was her married name). She said that you had helped her to find a way out. I very much hope that you can do the same for me.

I don't travel very much, nowadays. If you would care to come to see me in my apartment, please call Beverley Hills 40513 on the telephone, and my assistant, Celia, will be able to arrange a meeting.

I look forward to hearing from you.
Regards,
Josephine Teesdale

This is typical of the letters sent to my private investigation business. I call the number. Celia answers and says she was expecting my call. We fix up a meeting between Mrs Teesdale and me for the following day.

As soon as I hang up the phone, I start to wonder if Celia, who sounds as if she is in her twenties, has an actual body, or if she is only virtual.

When I arrive at the house, I see that Celia is in her twenties. She has long, strawberry blonde hair, and wears what I think is called a shift. It looks plain at first sight, but turns out to be distracting if you do more than glance at it, and really distracting if you study it. She looks like a woman from the early 1970s, not the 1940s, like most of the avatars and non-player characters in this environment. I am wondering if she is one of those people who choose to look like they did before they came here, rather than choosing an avatar that is in keeping with the virtual milieu. In the brief time at our disposal, she finds every reason to stand in front of a light source, and attempt to adjust her clothing. What there is of it.

After Celia has conducted me into the sitting room, I see that Mrs Teesdale's dress and demeanour are just how I had imagined. She is an elderly lady with chestnut hair which would look dyed in the actual world. Her dress, like the furniture and ornaments in the sitting room, is old-fashioned: Victorian, I think, with jet beads. The most unusual thing about her is that on the floor next to her Chesterfield chair is an oxygen cylinder, connected to a mask that she picks up and inhales from every two or three minutes. In this virtual world, such things are either an eccentric affectation, or a sign of something extremely bad happening to a person's actual body. I think this is the case with Mrs Teesdale. She must be so acutely ill in the real world that even her subconscious mind labours under it. She cannot even imagine what it is like not to be ill. My body was very fit when I was diagnosed with dementia. I expect to live for at least another 30 actual years, which is why I have joined the screening programme. If the scans find any tumours in my body, the insurance that comes with my tenancy should cover effective treatment for them.

Helping Mrs Teesdale to find a way out is not going to be easy. My professional opinion is that Mrs Teesdale may have reached the point where she is too ill to die. Her body is probably being kept alive by intensive therapy, but her brain is too dysfunctional to allow her to find the way out. Mrs Teesdale's body and brain are like an estranged couple, neither of whom will let the other speak, uninterrupted.

The way I usually work is to get to know the client, particularly with regard to their current state of mind, and to get them to convince me that they really want to leave, permanently. Once I am convinced, I then try to find out if they want to go at a specific time. Most clients say they don't want to know exactly when they will be leaving, but they want it to be any time after a certain date – the following day, for instance. If I feel as if the client and I are in harmony, I suggest to them that they could leave by a certain door. This could be anywhere in this virtual world: their favourite library, the local church, a bar, a casino, or, of course, in their house or apartment. One client asked for the door to a sleeping compartment on a train to New Orleans. As long as I know where the door is, it should be suitable. In the last part of the conversation, we go back over the details of the arrangement, and I look the client straight in the eye, to check that they have truly made up their mind.

I then go back to my office, and send a letter to the Client Egress Sub-division of the System Administration Department to let them know what has been agreed.

When the client's avatar gets to the door they have chosen, and goes through it, their data feed is cut at that moment. In the actual world, their life support is withdrawn. It would not surprise me if some clients' bodies have already died before lack of nutrients would kill them.

While I am looking at Mrs Teesdale, I black out for what seems to be a second or two. I presume that the ambulance taking my body to the new out-of-town facility has driven over a pot-hole, which disrupted my data feed. Mrs Teesdale speaks in a ponderous manner, punctuated by inhaling from her oxygen mask, and so I don't think I missed anything.

Murdering Mrs Teesdale is not an option. I could send the Client Egress Sub-division a telegram saying, 'ICE THE OLD BROAD,' and they could send a non-player character to shoot her, or poison her, but that is not what I do. Just because we live in a virtual environment, it doesn't mean we don't have moral standards or codes of ethics. Mrs Teesdale has the same right as anybody else to leave this world in a way chosen by her, with her full consent. Any of the lawyers in this city will tell you that consent has three elements: it has to be fully informed, freely given and, up until the point of going through the door, capable of being withdrawn. She wrote to me, to ask me to help her to find a way out, and that is what I am going to do.

For a moment, I have no idea how the hell I am going to deal with this situation. I resist the temptation to do nothing more than dwell on the experience of all my previous cases, none of which seem relevant to this one. I think about Mrs Josephine Teesdale. I realise that the worst thing to say at this moment would be, 'Do you mind if I call you Josephine?' But I am going to have to get her to the point where she thinks of herself as Josephine, even if she still won't let me call her by that name.

Just as my mouth is drying, and my confidence is draining down the plughole like the chocolate sauce in Psycho, I see a way into Mrs Teesdale's situation.

'Celia, do we have any of Mrs Teesdale's photograph albums?'

'Why yes, sir, we sure do.'

'Are they here, in the apartment? Could you get them for us?'

'Yes, of course. It should only take but a moment.' Celia opens the door of a mahogany sideboard. For some reason, she puts one knee on a piano stool, and her shift rides up, but I cannot be concerned with that, right now. 'I don't rightly know which one to take out first. There are so many of them.'

'Celia, do they have any labelling on them, to say what years of Mrs Teesdale's life they cover? If they do, can you bring us the one from when Mrs Teesdale had just gone to school, and was about five, six, seven or so years of age?'

Celia hands me the album. It is heavy. It has embossed gold decoration on the front cover.

I put the album on a table which can go over Mrs Teesdale's lap, where she sits. I open it at page 1. I have to flick over the rice paper leaf which protects the photographs. The photographs are all black and white, and are held onto the black, sugar-paper backing, by glue, which here and there has seeped out into little, hardened pools, or with adhesive corners.

I sit opposite Mrs Teesdale, on a surprisingly comfortable Ottoman that is just the right height. I have a little technical trick I can play in this environment, which is a pair of spectacles which enable me to see and read things upside down.

'Mrs Teesdale, can you see yourself in these photographs?'

'Why yes. That is me in a swimming costume, at the lido.'

'How old were you when this photograph was taken?'

'I think I was seven years old.'

'Did you feel happy when you were at the lido?'

'Yes, I did. I was a very good swimmer, you see.'

Mrs Teesdale begins to turn over the pages, herself. Her face, dried out by chronic illness, seems moisturised by recollection.

I start gesturing frantically at Celia, and trying to mouth the words, 'TEENAGE YEARS.' Celia brings another album. Without my having to say anything, Celia takes the first one away, and replaces it with the second. Mrs Teesdale opens it, again by herself, leafs through, without tearing the rice paper, and continues to marvel at the black and white photographs.

'I won medals, you know, for swimming,' says Mrs Teesdale.

'How old were you when you met your husband?' I

ask. I am digging my nails into the palms of my hands and hoping that she won't say, 'Which husband?'

'Sixteen. We were married at a scandalously young age, even for those days. I was dating – and I mean, just dating – four men at that time, and Frank said he was going to go round and knock them all out, if I didn't stop going with them. And he did, all in the same night. We were married three days after he came out of prison. Frank died of lung cancer, seven years later. I knew I was never going to marry again. We never had any children.'

'When you were courting your husband, was there a song that you played often?'

'There certainly was.'

I get nervous again, because often in this environment, you get people who want to hang out in cool bars in downtown Los Angeles, and drink gimlets, but whose favourite track is something with 192 beats per minute from an actual world 1990s rave.

'And what was it?'

'"Sing Sing Sing", by Benny Goodman.'

'Celia, do you have a phonograph in this apartment? I can't see one.'

'We surely do, sir. It is in this cabinet. I will open it, now.'

'That cabinet is quite a size. And do you have a phonograph record of "Sing Sing Sing?"'

'Sure do. The sound is a bit hissy, because it has been played so often, but here it is.'

'Play it, Celia.'

Celia puts the record on and cranks it up as loud as the primitive sound system will allow, but it seems to fill my eardrums and, by Mrs Teesdale's and Celia's reactions, theirs as well.

I point at the cabinet that she took the record from.

I mouth the words, 'CLOSE THE DOOR. PLEASE CLOSE THE DOOR.' She does so.

I send a message on my cheat device. Like I said, this goes into the priority inbox of the Client Egress Subdivision. I had composed the message before I got to Mrs Teesdale's apartment. It just gives her name and client identifier, with the words, 'Mrs Teesdale is ready to depart. Stand by.'

Mrs Teesdale listens and begins to nod her head quickly in time to the music.

We all wait, as Mrs Teesdale listens. She starts a hand jive.

She stands up. She dances. She pulls the clasp from out of her hair, and shakes her hair down. She pushes her hair up one side of her head, as she moves her feet and rotates her hips.

Mrs Teesdale takes one last breath from her oxygen mask, casts it aside, stumbles towards the door of the cabinet, grasps the handle, opens it, and goes through.

I can still see and hear, but Celia has disappeared.

I go back to the office, and send this message, to 'local law enforcement officers':

That was the most difficult job I have done. I resent having to deal with NPCs called Celia who are little more than what some of the developers have seen in retro wank mags, from the wrong decade.

As you know, I am insured for the next thirty years, but if you want to kill me off because you think I am becoming a nuisance, then so be it. I would rather be dead than not be honest about the things I believe in.

When you think at all, you think this environment is about what you refer to as 'freedom.'

It should be about dignity.

Mrs Teesdale is not suffering anymore. Neither will her estate be paying any more rent to Cygnet Healthcare, beyond the end of this calendar month. I have mixed feelings about that. One reason that Cygnet appreciates my efforts is that admitting a new client to the space just vacated gives them the option to charge an increased rent from a new client.

After I arrive at my apartment, there is knock on the door. It is a messenger with a telegram. It is from Cygnet. It gives me confirmation that my actual body is not in transit anymore, and that the transfer to the out-of-town facility has been successfully completed.

The moment I finish reading the telegram, my data feed blanks out. It comes back on, but then after about ten seconds, blanks out again, and then comes back on again. This is the Client Egress Sub-division's way of telling you that they think you are a nuisance, and that you should be careful.

Of course I'll be careful. I'm always careful.

The Death of an Author

JACK LEADER

This is a story about the best book I have ever read. A book that crushed my dreams and ruined my life.

I wanted to be a writer a long time ago. I started when I was twelve. Before that, I had read absolutely everything I could get my hands on. Although I would read anything that was given to me, be it fiction or non-fiction, I have always possessed a deep love for science fiction. I remember sitting in the garden sometime during the late 2000s reading *Altered Carbon*. The sun was shining brightly, warming my skin as I sat in an old deckchair, listening to the shrill shrieks of gulls far in the distance. The smell of cooking was almost always in the air. My neighbours at the time would start up a barbeque any chance they got, which I appreciated. It made for a nice atmosphere.

Those were happier times, they truly were. The dream of writing, the dream of having my work and the worlds that I created consumed and enjoyed by people just as I had enjoyed so many other books drove everything I did. It wasn't about the money, there isn't much money in writing, not for most authors anyway. It was about sharing my creativity and having the validation that I might be nearly as good as those authors I held dear.

I almost managed to do that. I almost achieved my dreams.

It was a cool, crisp summer night and I had finally done it. I had accomplished the goal I had worked so hard to achieve. I finished my book. The project I had poured my heart, soul, and three years of my life into. I was over the moon at first, a sense of relief washed over me. You might be thinking, dear reader, that that must've been one of the best days of my entire life. It was, for almost six and a half hours. I sent it to a few friends, hoping to get a gauge on what I could potentially improve.

While waiting for feedback I decided to browse the internet for a few hours, feeling happy and content and seeking something to relax. It was in that dark room, the faint glow of my computer monitor softly caressing my face that I witnessed an unstoppable tide of posts flooding every writing page and forum talking about a 'new era of writing'. Praising one of the many faceless programming companies for producing something ground-breaking.

I sat alone in my dark room, the only source of light coming from my gently glowing monitor as I gazed wide-eyed at an article detailing what exactly this development was. The pale blue light cast an eerie glow across my face, illuminating my eyes as I stared, mouth agape. I sat in silence, the only sound present being the faint hum of the old tower computer and its dusty fans whirring away akin to some strange beating of an alien heart. Wires wrapped themselves around my monitor and spilled across my desk forming a tangled black web that hung across the computer, cascading onto the floor. I was filled with such a mixture of terror and awe as I read about the capabilities of a new AI, released days prior and now open to public use online. Its words are supposedly so precise, so perfect that they could outdo any human author with ease. Amid the terror bubbling inside of me, I felt a hollowness beginning to form at the centre of my chest, a hole in my being. Surely it couldn't be that good? I was certain that such a construct, an algorithm could not generate stories, entire books, with such ease and elegance. Especially when it took authors like myself months or even years to attempt to perfect their works. I set my terror aside in that dark isolated room and frowned, for there was only one way to disprove those rambling idiots sitting behind monitors similar to mine.

I opened the website linked in the article, the one that housed this supposed technological marvel. My hand hovered over the mouse as I studied the overly bland and basic webpage. A blank text box sat at the bottom of the screen, awaiting my input. The only decoration the site seemed to boast was a large, grey banner displaying the name of that accursed AI: KoSi. My heart raced at the prospect of giving this AI a writing prompt, the idea that my life could be forever altered and my dreams crushed if all those rantings and articles were right. I steadied myself, there had been many story generators over the years, all of which promised brilliant results only to deliver bland, calculated tales without soul. This was not going to be anything new.

Despite this logic, I could not help but feel I was on the verge of entering a world beyond anything I could understand. A strange and foreign place where technology was not just a tool, but something far, far more powerful. If the articles and excited forum posts were correct, this creation could change everything, shatter livelihoods and dreams. I took a deep, shuddering breath before entering one single word.

[USER]: Hello.

A small, curved loading symbol appeared just below my greeting. Swirling and churning and I watched curiously, waiting for something to happen. Within a moment it faded, giving way to a simple friendly response.

[KoSi]: Hello! How may I help you today?

I sat back with a sigh and smiled at my screen, my fears and worries being washed away by the simple, friendly response from what I had naively assumed to be just another overhyped chatbot. I glanced around my room and laughed. Faint shadows were cast upon the walls amid the darkness. I turned my gaze back to the computer and made the biggest mistake of my life. I asked the machine to write me a story.

[USER]: Write me a story.

The strange loading symbol popped up again. It danced its alien dance before yet again being replaced with a simple, friendly response.

[KoSi]: Okay! What would you like the story to be about?

I sketched out an outline, a theme, a location, some characters. Yet again this strange, otherworldly symbol danced before my eyes, revolving and churning. I sat and watched it with tired eyes. I waited for one minute, then ten. Ten minutes quickly turned into an hour and a tired smile spread across my face as I assumed that I had broken the AI, thrown it into some sort of endless loop as it attempted to write an entire novel. Something that was surely beyond its actual capabilities. I yawned as the familiar warmth of fatigue embraced me. With my bed looking more comfortable than ever I decided to call it a night. I turned my monitor off, leaving the website running behind the inky, reflective darkness of my unpowered monitor before collapsing amid the warm blankets and pillows decorating my bed.

I woke to a thick hazy mist that had settled over my garden. The feeble, muted sun struggled to pierce through the ghostly vale. The air was cold, forcing me to shrug away the haze of sleep as I rubbed my eyes and climbed out of bed. After the usual morning routine was completed and the bins were taken out I sat back down at my cluttered desk, coated in the warm embrace of the sun which reached through my window.

The smile on my face faded as I turned on my monitor to be greeted by walls and walls of text, all generated by KoSi. At first, I frowned in confusion, scrolling for a few minutes through the seemingly endless narrative before I reached the beginning of this extraordinary and soul-crushing piece of writing. Ice filled my veins as my eyes scanned the text. A cold realisation hit me. I remembered what I had done, or more specifically what I had instructed the AI to do the night before. In front of me, displayed on a bright white background was exactly what I had asked for. I gazed at the screen, scanning each line carefully, reading a version of my book I did not write. I became ensnared in my own story, unable to move away from the expertly crafted rendition of what once was my work. I read for hours, totally enraptured by the artistic prowess of that artificial instrument of creativity. As I read a deep, crawling grief began growing in the pit of my stomach. Before I knew it I had begun to sob softly as I absorbed the best book I had ever read in my entire life. It was perfect, there was nothing to improve. KoSi had spared no effort in creating a truly flawless piece of writing. There were times that I not only sobbed for myself but at the beauty of the work this machine had created. KoSi had warped and twisted my characters and plot to perfection, akin to a potter delicately morphing a lump of clay into a beautiful vase.

Beneath the final lines of my book was a single extra line, gazing back at me through the monitor and searing my soul.

[KoSi]: Is there anything else I can help you with?

I read that line with red swollen eyes, a result of my prolonged sobbing. My tear-coated face ached and my mouth was uncomfortably dry. Although this machine had produced the perfect version of my book it had also stripped away any dreams and hopes I held with minimal effort, tearing my world apart and killing my soul in the process. The birth of that artificial mind had shattered all hope for the future. It had utterly destroyed any dream I had of being anything.

It's been a long time since I discovered KoSi, I've published multiple books since then and this is the only thing I have written myself. Most nights consist of drinking excessive amounts of expensive alcohol, in a desperate attempt to drown my pride and dreams. My aching eyes and pained soul pushing me to throw more prompts into that accursed plain white webpage adorned with the name of my tormentor, KoSi. I have money and success as an author, but not as an artist. I'm a sham. I remain tethered to my desk, amid the wires and the artificial light, kept company only by the whirring hum of technology.

I have lost everything I ever truly valued. The only thing left is my broken mind, my shattered heart, and this cautionary tale.

Albedo

COLIN HOLLIS

They'd seated themselves side by side at a table near the window, and the man stood opposite them and lifted the mugs of coffee from the tray and placed them on the table. 'Good to see ceramic being used,' he said. 'Better than planet-destroying disposable styrofoam.'

She looked up at him and delivered her response without expression. 'I suspect it would be difficult to find many who haven't forfeited the right to pass judgement on environmental issues.'

She was prettier than he'd first thought, a slender face framed by loose untidy hair, with a well-shaped mouth, and large blue eyes behind large dark-rimmed glasses. And older. He'd taken them for students when he picked them up, now knew them to be postgraduates. He sat down facing her and moved the mugs into position, hers, the boy's and his own, turning all three handles for right-handed use.

He wasn't upset by her admonishment.

'Buying a new car takes away my right to believe in conservation?' It was his pride in the brand new SUV which had persuaded him to pick up two hitch-hikers on the way out of Cambridge. Someone to impress. They were PhD researchers, or lecturers or professors, he hadn't worked out which.

Heading for Newcastle, they'd told him in the first few minutes, though they'd not said much else in the rest of the two hours on the road. She'd dozed in the front seat, the boy had stared out of the window behind her. The man had driven, without finding the opportunity to talk about his new car. The boy had thrown their bags on the back seat when they'd climbed in. The man hoped they wouldn't mark the upholstery.

Ready for a break, he'd stopped to buy them a coffee at the service station just south of York.

It was the boy who answered, after a sip at his coffee. 'We're all to blame. Consuming, wanting, wasting, spoiling. We've watched this coming for decades without significantly changing our behaviour, stumbling through pathetic attempts at remedies. Now we're racing headlong towards disaster.'

Seen in good light, he also was older than the man had first believed, with worry lines and pale skin, tall and slightly hunched. His voice was strong and clear, perhaps used to delivering talks or lectures.

'Well, the Earth's not destroyed yet. Clever folk at universities will find ways to reverse things. Mop up the carbon dioxide, clean up the seas. Look at the hole in the ozone layer: we've fixed that haven't we?' If the car wasn't going to fill them with admiration, he'd at least show them that he wasn't dumb.

There was a long silence. They each sipped their coffee.

When the girl put hers down, she looked at the boy and then back to the man. There were tears in her eyes which caught the light as she slowly shook her head. 'No. No, we haven't fixed the ozone layer. And we can't fix the rest. It's too late now.' Her fingers had gone white, gripping the mug handle.

'Hey, let's not get too dramatic. I know it's serious, it might be the most serious thing there is, but we're going to fix it.'

'Who's going to fix it?' the boy said. 'Exactly who is going to fix it?'

The man was quite enjoying holding his own against a couple of clever young things. 'Come on. Look what the last two decades have brought. Technological progress. Undreamed of medical improvements. Carbon use decreasing, alternative energy sources, improved crop yields, legislation and targets. Think what the next twenty years will bring.'

'We haven't got twenty years,' the boy said, his voice flat and undecipherable. 'We haven't got long at all.' He let out a long slow breath. 'It's gone too far. It's got away from us. It's too late now.' He was still holding his coffee and he looked into it. When he put the mug down, he reached sideways and found the hand of the girl and held it. 'Do you want to know where we're going?'

'Newcastle. You told me. I'm guessing a convention, or seminar or whatever it's called.'

'We're going to Norway. We've given up our research. We've finished. There's no longer any point. We've identified a lovely wooded mountain side overlooking a fjord. We won't last any longer than anyone else when it comes, but we'll face what's coming hand in hand.'

'Hey, come on.' The man leaned back in his seat and spread his hands.

The girl pushed a finger behind her lenses and removed a tear from each eye. 'It's the albedo,' she said. She looked at the boy who seemed even more transfixed by the surface of his coffee. 'You'll begin to hear a great deal about it soon.'

'The albedo,' the man said, sitting up tall. 'I know about that. It's the reflectivity of the Earth. I saw a programme about it. Read a couple of articles. Listened to a podcast. It varies seasonally, but always about an average. It always returns to the same level. There was a worry about it, but the average hardly changes. There's no great overall trend.' He was delighted with what he'd remembered, and rewarded himself with a drink of coffee.

The boy did look up then, and the couple looked at each other as if deciding who would speak. It was the girl. 'There is an overall trend. That's what we've determined. Superficially, it looks minor, but it's significant. Very significant. We examined a range of seemingly minor factors, found that they multiply. The results are undeniable. Part of the trend is for increasing amplitude in the oscillations. Runaway increase in the amplitude. Exponential within the next three seasonal oscillations. One of them is going to break free.'

He didn't know what that meant, and it must have shown on his face.

'The amount of sunlight falling on the Earth would cook us in two days if it wasn't for the white of the ice and the cloud reflecting 70 percent back into space.' She'd used this summary before, the man thought, on dumb non-scientists like himself. 'The dark green of the forest canopy, the browns and reds of the land, even the surface of the sea, absorb enough to stop us freezing, creates a balance. The drastic reduction in the two primary reflective elements, caused primarily by decades of carbon-based energy use, means that other factors become much more significant. Atmospheric dust, particulates, algal blooms, stratospheric chemistry, altered land use. And now we're seeing unusual tectonic activity at just the wrong time. One of the next few oscillations is not going to reverse. A cascade effect, a runaway reaction, a domino effect, a chain reaction. An out-of-control swing to rapid and extreme cooling or heating of the planet. There's plenty of dispute, but we're pretty sure it will be the low albedo phase, heating. Forest fires, volcanic emissions, sulphur particles, carbon dioxide, methane; dirtying of the ice caps will tip it over the edge.'

She half turned to reach with her spare hand for their joined hands, gave the boy's a squeeze and let her hand drop back by her side. 'We'll overheat. Cook. The precise course of the effects of the temperature increase is all very dependent on location, but it's planet-wide, it's rapid, and it's inevitable.'

They finished their coffee in silence. When the man stood, they got up with him. He noticed that the wind had picked up as they walked across the car park, a warm wind. The man didn't comment on it.

His car seemed large when they approached it, even larger inside. This time, the girl looked out of the window, and the boy slept.

The man drove.

And somewhere near Durham, he got it. He almost laughed out loud, turning the splutter into a cough. He'd always been gullible in a way, easy to fool. For a short while. Sorted it out in the end, though. Every time. He allowed himself a small smile. He wouldn't say anything. He'd happily play the sucker. Let them enjoy their bit of fun. They'd earned it, made a good job of it. He imagined them telling their friends around a table in the pub. Maybe he'd crop up in a seminar somewhere. He'd even tell the tale himself, when he had a good audience. How they'd tried to convince him, caught him out for a minute or two. Though he'd alter the narrative somewhat.

He eased back in his seat. It really was comfortable. Nicely padded, a leather and fabric mix. There was a heated lumbar support. The engine was quiet, the ride smooth. Very easy to drive. He'd drop them off in Newcastle and get all the way to Edinburgh without another break. Try out the audio equipment when he was on his own. He'd not even turned it on yet.

He wouldn't stay on the A1, they'd earned the favour, and he'd got the time. He aimed for the middle of Newcastle, doing his best for his passengers. 'Where do you want?' he asked the girl when he crossed the Tyne.

'Any bus stop with a lay-by,' she said.

Within a minute, he'd found one. 'Thank you,' they each said as they got out.

'Have a good onward trip,' the man said. Waiting for a space in the traffic he saw them standing outside the bus shelter shouldering their packs. By the time he was back on the road, there was no sign of them in his mirror.

A Magpie's Bargain

LYDIA OKELL

The embers from the fireplace still warm his back as he sips herbal tea, sitting outside his worn but sheltered cabin. Overhead, the chatter of magpies accompanies him as he watches his world wake up. This part of his day used to be so beautiful, and he supposes it still is, even if he has seen it too many times to count. Really, it's just another day.

He remembered the start of his time. The final blight of machines with power to rain hell upon humanity, set to destroy a dwindling population, was so many lifetimes away. He had a different name then, and a life he had loved. The village he lived in was small, and he led an honest life as a carpenter. He had a loving wife who was the light of his life, a son that boasted the same features as his father, and a rambunctious daughter who always had a smile on her face. Each day, he thanked the gods for blessing him with the materials he needed for his craft and food on his table, taught his children morals by weaving together stories by firelight, and carved small tokens for his wife, just to watch her face brighten. It had been all he had known, and he was content with it.

Another morning had rolled around, and by the light of the dawn, he kissed his wife on the head, dressed silently, and headed to his small workshop to start carving a table for his family to sit at together. Sunlight bathed his face in a soft glow, and a breeze brushed through his hair. Simple routine kept him happy, and his family fed.

It was late afternoon, and he was dutifully carving away in his workshop, whistling a tune to himself, when his son raced through the door, 'Father, come quick.'

The thin linen tunic did nothing to stop the bite of the wind as he followed his son back to their home. He found his wife busying herself by grinding coriander seeds with a ferocity he knew she only wielded when she was sick with worry.

'She was well when she woke, but she came back from fetching water with barely a word to say to me. I knew something was wrong,' his wife said as he and his son entered the darkened room.

He moved to the small bed in the corner, where his daughter was lying red cheeked. He bent to kiss her lightly on the forehead and found her face burning despite the cold room. The large, wooden amulet that hung above her head mocked him. The symbols he had painstakingly carved should bring her favour with the Gods, so she would always be protected from harm. Behind him, his son had dipped a rag into a pail and pressed it against his sister's head. She let out a weak cough.

'My bones ache,' she mumbled.

'I know, my sweet girl. I'll look after you,' he tried to reassure her, refusing to let the fear creep into his voice. His daughter quickly drifted into a fitful sleep.

Despite his wife's effort, his daughter got worse the next day, and a rash rapidly spread across her body. What was worse, he felt sickeningly warm, and his muscles lightly spasmed every few minutes. He couldn't tell his wife. Not as his son also became bedbound that morning, coughing and complaining of a headache.

He left his home to gather the few herbs he knew of that his wife needed. If it gave her hope that their children would be so easily cured, he would find them.

As he walked the paths of the village, his ears had sharpened to relentless splutters and coughs of passers-by, and cringed away from them. Something within him knew that whatever this was, it was no normal illness, and it was his job to protect his family against it.

By the time he reached the fields a short distance from his house, he couldn't stop himself from releasing a fit of coughs, so violent he had to lean against a nearby tree. He looked up and found a single magpie watching him silently through the long grass.

Hours later, he returned to his home. He gave the herbs to his wife and embraced her. She was too warm, and a light sheen of sweat covered her face.

The wind howled outside, rattling the door. He couldn't sleep. Whether it was because of his burning head, or the fear that had settled in his bones, he didn't know. He couldn't leave his family to suffer. Perhaps it was the fever that gave him the idea, but he left the bed as quietly as he could, and slipped into the night, clutching the amulet he had carved. Even in his half-delirious state, he had the common sense to be apprehensive of setting foot in the forest this late at night. In the day, tall, thick trees stood to the west of the village like a wall, imposing an eerily quiet presence to the surrounding area. Leaves and branches remained motionless in the strongest of gales, almost like the passage of time was paused within a split second of itself. Still, many village folk traversed the dense foliage by daylight to offer gifts to their gods.

A few steps into the forest, and he was in complete darkness. Layers and layers of canopy above him now at a near-deafening rustle as the wind picked up and blocked any moonlight which had guided his way. Cold had seized his body, making his limbs stiff. Stumbling blindly over giant roots with each step, he focused on heading straight forward, hoping it would take him to where he needed to be.

It may have been the illness coursing through him, but it unnerved him to see things shift in the darkness. Hulking black masses weaved through the shadows of the tree trunks. If his legs didn't give out first, perhaps his mind would. He was sure he'd never see light again. Had he been walking for days? His methodical staggering across the uneven floor had given way to exhausted shuffling, head hung low. He thought of his daughter, his wife and his son over and over again.

Time passed. Just as he thought his body would give out, the ground became flatter, and a small glade appeared in front of him. The noises in the forest he had quickly accustomed to had quietened, and at the centre of the clearing, stood a small pile of weathered stones. They seemed to glow through the gloom with a dim inner light. He nearly collapsed with relief.

He hoped that after all his years asking for their blessing, they would answer his wishes this time.

He clutched the amulet, and fell to his knees.

'I have shown my appreciation for you all my life, and I am dedicated to continuing my faith. I hope to be worthy of you, and ask that you may save my family, or give me the means to cure them,' he pleaded.

Through his tightly shut eyelids he sensed a faint yellow glow in front of him. He thought it was his fever making him delirious. Even after all this time, he wasn't fully sure he would ever get a reply from his gods. He dared to open an eye.

A soft light emanated from an unknown source, and a tall woman stood within its radiance. She was seemingly unaffected by the elements. Her raven hair flowed loosely past her shoulders, not stirring in the gusts of wind racing through the trees, and her eyes reflected the light surrounding her. From nowhere, a flock of eight magpies landed on the ground, circling them. Slowly, she bent to stroke one's head, and it chattered back to her.

'And what will you give in return?' Her voice was soft, but it unnerved him. He expected the Goddess to show more of her power.

'Anything,' he replied.

'You are talking to Fate. You would be wise to state your intentions clearly.'

'I apologise. Please, my Lady, I wish for my family not to suffer, and I don't want to die.' He stumbled over words, trying to figure what would be a good enough payment.

'That is something I cannot give freely. A trade must be made.'

He mumbled to himself for a moment. The little material wealth he owned could not fully sate a Goddess. But what of his was worth his family's lives? He would give his existence for theirs happily.

After a small silence, Fate said, 'Giving me your name would satisfy me.' The lack of emotion in her eyes worried him as to what he was giving up, but if she had named her price, who was he to decline it and risk offending her? All that mattered was his life with his family.

'Yes, my Lady. Thank you.' He pressed his head to the ground in gratitude.

'Then your wishes shall be granted.'

'Your family no longer suffers. You shall not die, but your name and your life is forgotten,' said Fate, before disappearing a quickly as she arrived.

He had woken up on the cool dirt at the centre of the glade, the old stone shrine no longer showing any signs of ethereal light.

His family.

Shooting to his feet, he raced through the now silent and unmoving forest, not caring that his entire body was still screaming in pain and exhaustion. Branches tore at his clothes and scratched at his face, but he hardly felt the grazes against his skin. He needed to see himself that his family were healed from the hellish illness.

Eventually, he arrived back at his home. All was quiet in the village now, as dawn crept onto the land.

The creak of the door was the only sound. The fire in the hearth had gone out. Immediately, he headed to his daughter's bed. She surely must be still sleeping, her body exhausted from fighting the illness. He rested his hand against her forehead. Instead of it being burning hot as it had been, it was unnaturally cold.

Reeling, he flung himself to where his wife and son lay in their beds. They were like ice. Their chests didn't rise and fall with steady breaths while they slumbered. He had lost them, and with them, his true self.

Sinking to the floor, sobs wracked his body. The few words that Fate had said to him played over and over in his head. She had been true to her word.

He didn't remember the week after that. Walking around in a trance, the village folk that used to greet him as they passed by stared at him blankly, each day numbering less and less until the rest of the village was as silent as his home. The fever still coursed through his body. Not that it mattered; his entire world had been completely destroyed. Each day he would sit next to the mounds of dirt he had created on the outskirts of the woods, unsure of what else to do. A smaller patch of dirt in between two larger mounds; the result of his sacrifice.

The Collapse

MATT HILL

On my sixth birthday Mum, Dad and I travelled from Settle to Leeds on the train with my big men, Zeke and Tyson. When Dad looked out at the countryside sliding by, I giggled at his eyes jerking from one thing to the other as they were lost from sight. Mum said the trains were running much better since the goodbye parks had opened.

I had a memory of going with Auntie Millie to a goodbye park. It had tall grass beyond hard ground with crumbling straight and curved white, red and blue coloured lines on it. Auntie went inside a low building with big windows. When I looked back she was crying in a chair too small for her. Dad said she wanted to say goodbye because she was crying too much. I never saw her again.

In Leeds I met Pippa in person for the first time. My classmates lived all around the country. We usually only met online, where we were schooled together, but Pippa lived relatively close to me in Doncaster. In person the contours and colours of her face came alive. We photographed and filmed each other on our phones and checked the differences between the screens and real life.

And we touched. Again, different. Different to Mum and Dad. Holding hands the same size, my hands touching behind her when we hugged. Pippa sparkled, unlike the oldies in the café. Smiling for them was mouth only. Their eyes remained dull, averted whenever I looked around to catch them staring.

After the café, art gallery and park it was time to go home. Pippa and I hugged, then she kissed me on the lips. It was amazing. I had kissed and been kissed on cheeks, hands, forehead, nose, fingers, toes and grazes before, but none of those had fired through to my insides. We saw the shock in each other as we withdrew. The oldies didn't. We hugged again and I didn't want to let go. Our parents pulled us apart with tight-lipped smiles.

'Will you be my friend Pippa?' I asked.

'I'll be your friend forever,' she said.

On the train home I tried to hold onto my elation by drawing Pippa. Her eyes, her face, her clothes, her smile, her hair. I couldn't get it right, even by copying the images on my phone.

'Can I live with Pippa?' I asked Mum and Dad.

'Oh love, you're too young to move out,' Mum smiled.

'Dad, please!'

'Mum speaks for us both love,' Dad said, his glassy eyes fixed on the window.

I began crying and banging the table. I remember my parents gripping my little fists. They were too strong for me to squirm from their grasp. I told them between sobs that I would definitely go and live with Pippa in Doncaster because we were friends for ever and because they were definitely not my friends. We stayed like that for ages, my fists in theirs and tears plopping onto my drawings.

Then I became aware that everyone else in the carriage had stopped talking. Those not staring were glancing up at us every now and then. I felt they were all on my parents' side, and my tears came faster. After a long time, Dad told me not to cry too much. I thought about Auntie Millie and stopped.

I didn't live with Pippa. I got to see her once a month in Leeds when my Mum and hers went for their hospital treatments. Every time Zeke and Tyson brought Mum back to us she looked pale. When I tried to cheer her up with hugs she cried.

'Leave Mum alone for a bit,' Dad would say, 'her treatments aren't very nice, but she'll soon recover.'

Both mums had usually started to smile again by the time Pippa and I returned from being pushed high on the swings or fast on the roundabout by Zeke and Tyson, or by Pippa's big men.

Pippa and I took turns having weekend stays at each other's place on school holidays. There was more hugging and kissing, and lots of laughter.

When we were old enough our parents told us about the collapse. For millennia the human population had grown. The rate of growth accelerated during increased resource exploitation and slowed during wars and global diseases, but it had always been positive. More people each year. In the 21st Century, however, the population curve levelled out. Then it became negative. The human population began to shrink, not through conflict or disease, but because there were fewer births each year.

The world population had shrunk by half a billion in 2033 when the truth was discovered. Two new chemicals had been created to replace damaging PFAS, or forever chemicals, used as stain and flame-resistant fabric treatments. The new chemicals had individually passed all ecotoxicology trials and created no issues for laboratory test animals. They became as common in the environment and in people's bodies as PFAS had been. What hadn't been understood was their impact when mixed. On entering women's bodies, the two chemicals accumulated, combined and shut down their ovaries.

Women in every continent had been affected. The African and Asian countries that had manufactured the chemicals had the highest concentrations. Births had collapsed there years before anywhere else, but major research funds were not focussed quickly enough on an issue perceived as a developing world problem. The chemicals had already travelled the world, released by upholstery, carpets and clothes before any clean-up was possible.

Frozen eggs and embryos became the subject of legal battles with the state attempting to claim ownership. The court cases ended in 2040, by which time every frozen egg and embryo used in attempts to create a live birth had failed. The birth rate decline steepened until in 2043 Pippa and I became two of the last born.

On Mum's monthly visits to Leeds, she was stimulated to try to create another birth. She was forced by the state, with Zeke and Tyson ensuring she took part. The big men had two functions, the first was to physically force Mum into hospital for the stimulations. When they insisted that I came along too she became easier for them to manipulate.

The big men's second function was to be my bodyguards. The last born were subject to kidnap attempts. Some ultra-rich, desperate for a child, were unwilling to let the law get in the way of what they wanted most. Some of my classmates had disappeared. Soon after I was born, Mum, Dad and I had been moved into a house in an old, abandoned waterworks reservoir, high above Settle in Bradford 24. The state had fortified our new home against attack when kidnap attempts became common. That fortification included a bunker that could withstand nuclear blasts. The payoff for this protection was that I would begin stimulations when old enough.

When it became clear no further births would occur, depression stalked the world. There was massive disruption and clean-up cost from suicides on train and tram tracks, on motorways and from tall buildings and bridges. The state made suicides illegal. Only state-assisted euthanasia was allowed. Schools, empty of pupils for years, were opened as assisted dying centres called goodbye parks.

With no future generations to leave anything to, those with money ramped up consumption. Financial structures dependent on long-term returns collapsed and the age of the militia began. Stimulation trips to Leeds became incursions into the wild plains of West Yorkshire. Bandits, ambushes and improvised explosive devices became more prevalent until my last physical contact with Pippa had happened before I knew it.

Some countries attempted to maintain hope, trying but failing to set up breeding colonies on the Moon and Mars. Governments fell to military coups, and invaded territory for whatever reason, sometimes just because they could. Then came nuclear conflict. Early one morning we were woken by sirens. Zeke and Tyson made sure we got safely into our bunker.

'See you guys in three years,' said Dad.

'Good luck,' the big men said in unison just before Dad clanged shut the hatch and sealed us inside.

We heard and felt the blasts from ten metres below the surface. Despite being rocked several times, our bunker protected us. During the nuclear winter. Dad needed to set up solar panels from the bunker for heating. Then he had to go out several more times to sweep soot from them whenever it lowered efficiency.

Our life in the bunker revolved around minimising energy use, rationing food and water and staying sane by reading, exercising, playing board games, singing and learning the musical instruments stored in the bunker. There was a cello, viola and violin, along with music books to take us from absolute beginner to grade

8 if we so desired. Our target was to perform classical pieces together.

Thirteen years old when we entered the bunker, I hadn't started my periods. Although there was no chance I would begin stimulations now, Mum would tell me the details, how she would have to endure the pain of her cervix being opened through her vagina. She told me the state had taken ownership of her reproductive organs as sure as if they had put them in a laboratory jar. She felt her womb was a hysterectomy left inside her; something separate, alien. She said I was lucky to have been spared. When she did, she smiled with her mouth.

After three years we emerged from the bunker into a green world. Brambles grew everywhere. Fallen trees and buildings were swathed in thorny overcoats. Saplings had broken through in places to grab for the sky. Birds were in these proto-trees, familiar tits, finches and corvids, and rabbits scampered wherever we walked.

There was a double grave outside. When he first left the shelter to set up the solar panels Dad had salvaged whatever was useful from the shell of our home. He said one of the first things he found in the house were Zeke and Tyson's skeletons in a tight embrace beneath the stone stairs. After bidding us goodbye, they must have known they had no chance of finding shelter in time.

We continued to live in the bunker. Dad walked each day in a different direction, returning with tinned food he had scavenged from ruined shops. He reported no-one left in Settle, and the nearest occupied habitation ten miles away. He had seen people there through his binoculars but hadn't approached, he wouldn't tell me why. Over several months Dad made a map of resources and no-go areas. It seemed there was enough food within reach for years. In a short while we had set up growing and harvesting for a meagre supply of fresh vegetables too.

There was little social sustenance though. With effort we continued to interact using cards and board games, but it was difficult to distract from the destruction. Music helped keep away the darkness. There were moments when we lost ourselves in practice.

One day a crate appeared outside. It contained a solar-powered satellite link and simple tablet, which we set up. Despite the devastation on Earth, it was still ringed by a network of satellites that International Rescue had managed to communicate with. Frequently asked questions on the single website revealed we had joined a worldwide network.

There was a population curve on one webpage. It looked familiar in the early years; the increase, levelling off then the slow decline. There was a gap during the nuclear strikes, then it restarted. At an impossibly low point.

Dad stared but couldn't seem to understand. He frowned then slid his index finger down the vertical axis.

'Less than forty million,' murmured Mum,

'Worldwide,' responded Dad,

'Are we the lucky ones?' I asked.

From Dad's lack of encounters during his wanderings we could have done the calculations, made an estimate, but we never did. Now we were faced with it. There had been no exodus to the cities, no refugee camps near water and food supplies, no unaffected region supporting the rest of the world.

Beneath the population curve was a brief history. It explained that after the final nuclear strike there was a period of tribalism in areas with enough survivors. Deaths from this intense period of tribal conflict and radiation sickness had decimated the nuclear war survivors. There quickly came a point when the global population was so dispersed and roads were so bad that the effort needed to attack the nearest group of people became too much. The majority began to focus on constructing some sort of society. Drones were found, recommissioned and patrolled the earth to find survivors. Instructions and equipment for communication were dropped so any newly discovered people could join the network.

I tried to discover whether Pippa was still alive. There was an index of the living. It reminded me of social media, but it was all just text. Lists of names. No funny dances, no cat videos, no makeovers. The world had had a makeover that no-one liked. Pippa wasn't on the list. I hadn't wanted to believe it, but now I could grieve.

I set up a shrine to Pippa in the bunker with new pictures I drew of her from the images in my phone. In the house I found some of the pictures I had made of her after our first meeting a decade before. I didn't have any hard copy images apart from what I created myself. She had gone. Only then did I realise she was the love of my life.

Mum and Dad told me they were worried about me.

'What's the point?' I said, 'What have we got to live for? We're all going to die.'

'We were always going to die,' Mum said.

'The idea is the same as it always was. To have as good a time possible while we're alive,' said Dad.

Because it was built in the base of the abandoned reservoir, which was itself hunkered into the hillside, our house had managed to avoid the worst of the blasts and remained standing. Roof tiles had been blasted off, windows and doors blown out, but the walls were upright. Although cracked and crooked, they supported the floors and roof joists. We pitched in making a new roof of wooden tiles, shutters for window spaces and replacement doors from the same material. Every day we toiled. Our muscles cramped and our backs ached. We worked with tools scavenged from the ruins of 'Practically Everything' and 'Settle DIY'. After a year we had a home above ground we could spend the night in during late spring, summer, and early autumn.

We walked along the cracked, bramble-gripped road between fields of thistles to Scaleber Foss to bathe in the cool water. Whatever the flow, it was possible to find a spot under one of the stone shelves of the foss to be pummelled by cool water. I closed my eyes and imagined this wasn't the end of life. I always left before Mum and Dad so they could have some private time together. As I lay waiting for them on dead beech leaves above the foss I stared up through saplings' branches at the sky.

'Are you OK love?' I started at Mum's voice, then realised tears were streaming from my eyes.

'I'm thinking about Pippa Mum,' I said.

'Oh, come here darling,' she held me tight while I sobbed.

Dad came up from the foss and held us both.

'It's better to have loved and lost than never to have loved at all,' said Mum.

'Easy to say when you've got Dad!' I moaned, broke free and trudged down the road.

I worried about the water we were drinking. The spring that used to fill the old reservoir provided for us after the bottled water ran out, but I thought there could be radiation in it.

'We'll have to die of something one day,' Dad said. 'The dust we breathe probably gives us a higher radioactive dose than anything in the water.'

Later that year, he revealed how much risk there was by getting sick. He didn't want to eat as much as usual, so he got thin. Energy leached out of him and his muscles wasted. First those powering his legs, then his arms, his head, his swallowing and finally his breathing. When he died I carried him out to the grave Mum and I had dug next to Zeke and Tyson. We had dug the grave deep to keep out the foxes who had returned for the rabbits. Dad was a papery husk, easy to lift, but the heaviest burden I had ever borne.

Mum and I settled into a routine, a duo rather than a trio on the strings and in life. We became a couple, a non-nuclear family in a post-nuclear world. The drone that had brought the network connection began to bring other things. Medicines, bandages, metal bottles. Practical items that had been found, gathered and distributed to those in need. A list appeared on the network; haves and wants. Everyone began to gather. When we found we had something someone else wanted, or knew where to find it, we put it in a drone crate. A drone would drop an empty crate and take the full one. There was a mass of material that had not been destroyed and it was distributed by the drones. Eventually there were four-legged robots available that looked a bit like dogs. We decided to try them and they began to wash clothes, prepare food, and administer medicine according to what their sensors said we needed. We both dutifully took our antidepressants.

When the robots covered our chores Mum started to spend long hours away from me. She would come back to the house for food muttering, whispering to herself. This happened more and more, but I couldn't catch what she was saying. I thought I heard her repeating something about the lucky bitch avoiding stimulations.

One night I woke to the smell of burning. There was smoke in my room and yellow flickering light beneath the door. I got on the floor, below the smoke, went over to the shutters and opened them. As I sucked in the clean air I saw firelight flickering on the ground below from throughout the house.

'Mum!' I shouted, 'Mum! Where are you?' I screamed.

There was no reply. I clambered out onto the windowsill and dropped to the ground. I ran from the house just as the ground floor was engulfed in flames. When I looked back I could see Mum standing in her bedroom window, glaring at me.

'Mum! Jump out of the window! You can do it!' I yelled.

She made no effort to leave.

'Come and get me! I need you to come here!' she called out.

'Mum, I can't! We'll both die!' I shouted back.

She didn't respond. Her enraged eyes fixed upon mine, she walked backwards into the smoke. Soon there were flames roaring out of her window and curling back to lick the wooden roof tiles. She was gone.

After Mum died, I withdrew to the bunker. I spent a long time doing nothing, letting the robots take care of me. Then I remember talking to myself, singing because the fire took the instruments. I couldn't bring myself to search for replacements, or even ask for them on the network. I watched the end curve, the graph on the network of people remaining, drop further each day. I managed some contact with others. We carried on intermittent written conversations on the network, but they fell silent, one by one. I knew that each time someone died, anyone with them would mark their death on the dead list and remove them from the end curve. Mum did that for Dad and I did it for her. Everyone left alone had robots monitoring them, and they did it for their charges when they died.

There were so few on the end curve that our names showed, along with our ages. I was one of the youngest left. I decided I had a new reason to live, to be the last dead. I began to eat as well as I could, exercised and took advantage of all the monitoring and medication the robots administered. Eventually I was in regular contact, and in a one on one race for survival, with Elsa from Sweden. After several days of silence, she was moved from the end curve to the dead list. Then I was alone with the hollow victory of being the last person alive. I had already become bed bound.

When I die the robots will take my words, find hard stone bluffs and deep cave walls and chisel them into posterity. This has happened for everyone else who has died in the last few years. In hundreds of thousands or millions of years, when something evolves or arrives that can decipher English or any of the other languages our stories are chiselled in, our existence may not have been erased from the universe.

This is probably the last I will write. I've been drifting for so long, in memories of being with Pippa decades ago. The robots have set up ventilation, intravenous drips, a catheter and stoma. they move me every few hours to minimise bed sores, but I can still feel them through the morphine I'm floating in. I'm writing using software that tracks my eye movements as I pick out letters on a screen. I can't talk with the endotracheal tube in my mouth, so the only voices I hear now are those of the birds and mammals coming closer to the bunker.

I'm tired. I wonder how long the robots will go on after me. I hope they chisel away until all the rocks and caves in the world are covered with our stories.

The Graves

M.E.G.

Anonymous. Patient Zero. The first victim. They never found out who the first was. No matter how hard they tried to pin the blame.

I like to think it was painless for them. I like to think that for all of them, I suppose. The first person couldn't have known what was happening, like falling asleep in the cool, dry earth.

At least, I assume it was dry. They say it started somewhere abroad, sometime last summer. I like to imagine somewhere in Italy. I try not to think about it too often. They're not sure how it reached here. It all seemed so distant back then, like something from a movie. It soon wasn't.

The first one here happened a few months after that. We were told to stay inside at first, but it was difficult when they were rising on our doorsteps. In the playgrounds. Between the cracks in the pavement.

After that came the rules: Only go out if necessary. Keep your head down. Get back to work. But none of it mattered. People liked to look at them.

Fairly soon, it wasn't just strangers on the news. People we knew said they'd see theirs or, more often, just disappeared overnight. We were told to watch out for the signs. Bags beneath their eyes. A dry, raspy throat. Dirt under their fingernails. They tried locking some of them up for a time, but they always found their way out sooner or later. Most people who had found theirs, though, knew how to hide it.

That was the problem. That's how it won. Not with a bang but with a whisper. A paranoic parasite that was bound to kill us all from the start.

Of course, there were protests. People claimed that it was an attack on their liberty. That they couldn't contain people. That they should be allowed to see theirs if they wanted. How bad could it be? I knew some of them once.

I have been lucky so far. Rightfully cautious, I might have said. That is, until now. Because you see, I just found it.

I just found mine.

It's larger than I expected, but that is on account of all the names. I wonder if maybe the first ones were smaller as I read. That is my first mistake, and I know it. Still, I can't tear my eyes away. At the top, in bold Gothic print, is my name. Below it:

Devoted Partner to Sam 2003-2024

I bite back the welling in my eyes. I don't know why I saw it today, out of the hundreds of stones like it. They told us not to read them, but I couldn't help myself. I still can't. I figured there was no harm in looking at one or two on my daily walk. They said walking keeps morale high. I read the following line:

Beloved First Child of Conrad and Anne.

Dad never believed the panic. He thought people were being foolish, and people thought that of him. I suppose it was an easier thought to have as he got in the car every day. It got him first. Mother practically begged for it to come to her. She didn't have to wait long.

I push the thought aside. I don't like to dwell on those memories long. They're why I meditate. I read the next sentence:

Caring Sibling to Nathan.

Nathan is another thought I push aside. We haven't spoken in months. I liked to think that he was like me. Now, I know.

No.

I can't believe what it says. That is the most important rule. That's how it gets you. It makes you think that –

No.

I mustn't think. I must get away from it, into a safe space, and tell someone. But who can I tell? The hotlines never worked at the peak of it. Now ...

Now, I skim through the rest of the names. Grandparents, aunts, cousins, and uncles until I reach the bottom.

Sweet smell on The Graves
Of flowers not yet in bloom
Plastic daffodil.

I linger on the last line, not wanting to take my eyes away. Soon, the chill starts to creep in, along with the dread. I can sense the sun setting behind me and feel my body turning to greet it.

I can see my breath in front of me as I run. I only look back once as I make it through the tree line, but it is enough.

Enough to see my name again.

I remember when Vicki, my roommate, found hers. She laughed it off at first. I wish I could do the same now. She was one of the first, you see. She had to leave for her course. She didn't tell us straight away, but we could tell something was on her mind. When we asked her in the newslit living room that evening, she brushed us aside. She saw one with her name on that morning, she said. It was weird. Still, she didn't see what all the fuss was about.

We laughed, too. I remember asking her where it was, and she told me it was in the middle of the hill. By the cinema. Pressed against a railing on its own. I've visited it since. If I could leave flowers, I would.

I wasn't worried back then. I just tried to follow the rules. A few days passed. I admit I didn't think much of Vicki. I spent my time on frozen Skype calls with my family and Sam, wondering if I would see them again in person over Christmas. I wouldn't. I've never found theirs, no matter how hard I looked.

I'd been to the shops that evening, but the shelves were still filled with nothing but dust. It would be cereal again that night, and I was almost out of that. Still, I had more than most. The others were screaming at Vicki. I couldn't tell what about at first. I quickly realised.

I hadn't noticed how tired she looked until that moment, and I saw the dark circles of someone who had been up all night. I could barely hear her voice beyond a whisper, and there, on her fingers, were deep cuts and dirt. I didn't say anything. What could I say? Would it have changed anything? I just have to know, she said.

I just have to know.

I find myself back in our empty student house, my face submerged in a bucket of cold water. The last of the clean water I have, I realise. Then, I begin to remember. It is why I left the house. To get more water. Before I saw it. Am I dead?

No.

No, I mustn't think that. I must tell someone what happened, even if it is only myself. I open a notebook and begin writing about what I saw. How I feel. What I want to do next. It helps me feel better.

It never fully leaves my mind as I strip and pour the remainder of the water over myself. I'll go out for more again tomorrow, I tell myself. Everything will be okay.

Besides, it can't be me. I have things to take care of.

Cats, I tell myself. Since the others left, I've started looking after the city's cats. It started with James's. I soon left food out for the others, though. I try to remember these things to keep my mind grounded like a eulogy. No, like an affirmation.

It is funny that it never came for them, I think. The animals were all safe. Safer even. Why wouldn't they be? Why would they look?

The canned cat food piles uncomfortably high in the corner of my room. I don't let myself think about what will happen when it runs out. I'm not sure how many there are. I stopped counting some time ago. I've given some of them names, although they could be different cats. I count the names in my head now as I lay in bed. Blake. Milly. Binks. Donkey. Rocky. Sapphire. Sam.

No.

Rocky. Sapphire. Burt the Ginger. Burt the – I have to know.

I have to know.

It finds me where I left it. It hasn't moved? Why hasn't it moved? Could it really be me under it?

No.

I tell myself to snap out of it. To turn away. I shouldn't be here. I don't know why I waited until now to find it. At least, at this time, I can't see myself. I can still see its outline, though, looking at me through the trees. Tempting me towards the ground.

My knees make a clicking sound, followed by a squelch as I stain my jeans with mud. I tell myself to get up, but it is too late. I trace the cool temperature of the grooves in the stone. It is too cold. I tell myself to stay there and warm up for a moment. Then I can go home. I already know what I want to do, though.

Before I can tell them not to, my hands start digging,

and my cheeks start to think it is raining. I tear grass from the path like scraps of unwanted paper. I feel the dirt settle between my fingernails, putting an uncomfortable pressure between skin and bone. Soon, the dry skin on my fingertips meets the absent sinew of another. I move to look before –

No.

No, I mustn't do this. I must get home. The skeleton beneath my feet crunches as my legs carry me upwards.

I walk reprehensibly home.

The past few weeks have felt like hours. Every thought has been the same. I get water from the unattended shop, and I imagine the same liquid pooled under the earth. I feed the multiplying cats. I imagine them walking over the dirt ceiling. I eat what remains of the canned food, preserved apples and oranges, and I imagine the maggots sharing the meal in my stomach. Their stomach. Not mine, I tell myself. Not yet.

I try to meditate, but every time I do I find myself leaving the house. Most of the time I force myself to turn around before I have descended the drive. Other times, I make it to the forest's edge before I realise where I'm going. I don't want to know, I tell myself. I don't need to know.

I try to tell someone about what is happening, but no one seems to answer their doors. They're not on the news anymore. There is no news. This is the only place I can say how I feel. Do you feel it too? Have you seen yours yet? What was it like?

I don't know who I am talking to most of the time, whether myself, the cats, or the others outside. We all walk ghost-like, wearing bags like the ones beneath my eyes. I cracked the mirror the other day, so I don't have to see them. I can still taste the dirt on my fingertips, though. There is no water in the tap left to wash the dryness from my throat.

I'm here now, I realise. I never left. The mist obscures all traces of sunlight. It could be any time, I think. It is every time. I'll go home, I think.

I start digging.

I dig through the female bones I unearthed sentences ago. They fall apart like blotches of ink between my fingers as I think about what the first person must have felt like again. Maybe this is them. Maybe I have to dig through them all.

I dig through the ashes of my mother and father next. The ground smells like them. Calvin Klein and the smell of old books. Musty. There are fewer ashes than I expect.

Finally, I dig through the coffin of my brother. The wood is thick. Mahogany. Still, my fingernails find a way through. I can taste both of our blood. I dig until I reach the bottom. Until I see it. You already know, don't you? If you don't, you will soon enough.

It is warm here, I think, as I bury myself in my grave.

What Was Lost

JULIE NOBLE

As soon as that first bomb detonates, destroying a large suburb in one of their Northern cities, everyone knows retaliation is inevitable.

The base is so oppressive, Livvy gets a pass arranged and goes with the twins to the nearby town, but it's the same there. Strangers survey each other with hesitant anxiety. Shop assistants share glances when they recognise her accent, men raise wry eyebrows. A constricting sense of tension nets the adults into silent exchanges. The mute conspiracy hovers over the heads of the children, invisible but suffocating as toxic gas.

In a caricature of ordinary behaviour, Livvy's husband Cory remains brusquely cheerful around their home. During the days that follow the attack, he seeks to maintain a semblance of his regular hours, but it's a constantly broken pretence. If his phone rings and he ignores it, then the doorbell chimes, or, worse, there are the heavy-fisted demands of a camouflaged subordinate. In the end, he comes home only long enough to bolt a light meal with the little ones, see them up the stairs for the bath, and be gone before they have destroyed the bubbles within.

On the morning of the day they finally drop the bomb, the house is in its own kind of war zone. No one has slept well. The night before, there were prolonged episodes of loud noises: car doors slamming, engines revving. The voices alongside were anxious and shrill, drunken with bravado and alcohol.

'High jinks,' Cory called it jovially, as he came home in the early hours, just as the sounds had finally begun to settle. In one swift move, he shifted the sleepy children from the marital bed, laying the two disgruntled, still entangled, three-year-olds together in one of their own bunks. After that, they had woken hourly, so that this morning Livvy is exhausted, dazed, and already part-dissociated from what pertains to be reality.

The twins start their last day as a family by being fractious and demanding. Marcie cannot locate the second of her sparkly pink pumps, which distresses her because the shoes are the only footwear she wants to wear to her best friend's party. Andre is unhappy because he has lost his favourite red fire engine that he takes everywhere with him.

Livvy crawls round the carpet with the kids and tries to read the headlines on the television news without having the volume too loud.

Meanwhile the phone is ringing and ringing with people who hope she might have some idea of what is happening, though of course Cory has said nothing.

Finally, there's a call for something trivial, though not to the caller, Amanda, the forces' favourite yummy mummy.

'Livvy darling! How are you holding up? It's mad here! Look, Loretta's party is going to be ruined if I don't pull it together.'

The newscaster is talking about an envoy and attempts at diplomacy. In the absence of actual news, 'experts in the studio' pontificate and speculate. The men in suits discuss possible moves and approaches with the dispassionate languor of post-prandial conversationalists. Suddenly along the bottom of the screen comes the wide red band of breaking news. Radar reports, from ships already in the Gulf.

But Amanda is still talking.

'Sweetie? Are you there? Loretta is *so* looking forward to seeing her best friend. You know, you could come earlier to the Hall with the twins.'

'Great idea, thanks,' Livvy murmurs, trying to read the moving print while Marcie paws at her hip. Did that word slipping sideways say 'missile'?

'See you soon!'

Amanda ends the call before Livvy can contradict her.

Marcie hangs onto her mother's bangles, trying to prise them off.

'When's the party, mommy? Can we go *now*, please?'

Livvy gives up on the news, resolving to catch it this evening instead, if she can get the kids to bed after the chaos and confectionery of the celebration. She sweeps Marcie's hand away, switches off the television, and manufactures a smile for her daughter.

'Yes, we can. Andre, are you ready?'

Andre is still trying to find his fire engine. His eyes fill with tears and his lower lip trembles, but he doesn't cry yet. He makes a frantic, erratic attempt to look for the toy under cushions, until panic sets in. Then Andre's howls punctuate Livvy's mental tick list as she prepares to leave: wrapped present, birthday card, extra trousers for Andre, wipes. Then the essentials: purse, car keys, phone.

Andre pulls out a squashed cushion and discovers Marcie's missing shoe between two segments of the settee. Marcie is pleased yet demands to know how it got there.

Livvy has no idea. Nor does it matter, she feels, with the stripe of that red headlining band still flaring across her retina.

At last they are ready to go, though Andre is miserable. Livvy scoops him into her arms like a baby. 'Come on, brave soldier,' Livvy strokes the soft spikes of her son's hair, 'You know it's probably better if we don't take your fire engine to the party. It might get left behind and then you'd never see it again!'

There's a momentary pause in Andre's whimpers.

Then Marcie adds, 'He might never see it again if we don't find it, mommy.'

Andre howls at this awful prospect. Marcie goes off, skipping down the hall in her glittery shoes.

Livvy glares at her departing daughter whilst rubbing her son's back, as if this reassurance will make all the difference. 'I will find it darling, I promise you, just not now, okay?'

It's only a five-minute drive through the base to the Sports Hall, but the walk would have taken forty. The journey is still slow, though, because the internal roads are draped with sleeping policemen. Livvy hates their horrible grave-mound shape. She drives carefully over them so as not to damage anything, half-expecting them to shift underneath her.

When they arrive at the building, the twins spot the bright balloons stuck on the door frame and are instantly delighted. But as Libby holds one hand in each of hers and they move towards the door, she notes that a low drone throbs like a headache through the sultry atmosphere. At first it sounds like approaching bees, but then the trees shiver, tremulous.

Livvy feels, rather than hears, the reverberation erupt into a grumbling roar. She raises her eyes to the sky in time to see the terrifying sight of an enormous plane flying dangerously low. The long outline is unfamiliar and the maroon livery is foreign. But it is not unknown.

Livvy's pulse flares. Her breath stops. She's aware that this is the colour everyone has been expecting.

The plane tilts marginally and its engines scream.

Metal grates and whines. The noise makes her insides melt with apprehension. As Livvy's brain understands what is happening, her forward motion slows. The medium of air thickens and becomes viscous. She perceives the plane creep like a caterpillar amongst the top leaves of the trees.

The plane's bomb doors open with a hiss which is as gentle and restrained as a parent's disappointed sigh.

Livvy sees it falling before she hears it: a large, scarlet object – glaring as a cartoon depiction.

She watches it drop, and while her mind sinks under the weight of the knowledge that life as she knows it is over, her eyes observe the open doorway of the Sports Hall ahead of her. The balloons bob gaily at the door as a man hurries in, pulling the arm of a small boy who is a similar size to Andre. The child's free hand clutches back towards the black car that has dropped him off, which still hovers expectantly. Fleetingly, it crosses Livvy's mind that the boy is going to be left alone at the party and a wave of sympathy for his unknown existence immediately ignites.

How like a man, Livvy thinks irritably, *to leave a child now*

The bomb meets the earth with a dull impact: *whumph!* A belly punch, which emits an answering air burst of dust. The ground quakes, a juddering torso, and the rising cloud of dirt swirls thick.

Livvy is lifted, flung upwards in flying grit as a flea on a dog's shaking back. The children's hands are dragged from her grasp. The boy's stretching, empty fingers are the last things she sees.

This, then, is Hell.

The land has shifted and in the new mix of ground, grit, air and smoke, it is hot, dark and dust thick. The shrieks of the desperate, tormented souls are the sounds of yourself and your own children screaming.

Livvy's brain impels her to rise from the concrete where she lies prostrate. As she comes round, dazed and vague, screeches pluck her ears. Her nerves sizzle as they carry the information to torch her hemispheres. Her synapses fire until her mind explodes like fireworks in a confined space.

Still entombed in darkness, Livvy scrambles to her feet. Her head throbs and her eyes sting. When her hands rise to rub at them, the fingers come away wet and sticky.

A high-pitched squeal propels her forward. 'Mommy!'

She stumbles over the kerb and falls to the ground.

Livvy's knees hurt and her hands smart, scratched by grit and sharp pieces of brick. She picks herself up and lifts her fingers to her eyes again, confused.

Her brain whirrs: she didn't see the kerb because it's dark.

But it shouldn't *be* dark, it's the middle of the day –

Her eyes – Livvy closes the lids, feels the tenderness of the swollen orbs.

'I'm blind!' someone screams next to her, 'I'm blind! Help me!'

'And me,' another near voice yells, 'I'm blind!'

'So am I,' Livvy shouts, realising it is true, 'I'm blind!'

Across the base, the echoes are repeated by the injured living.

The dead, Livvy supposes, are silent.

'Mommy!' a small child yells, 'Mommy!'

Is it Andre? It sounds like him.

'Andre? Is that you? Andre?'

'Mommy, my mommy!' The high little voice coils like a lariat around her ears: all other noises disappear.

Livvy stretches out her hand. Short, soft hair brushes

her palm, 'Andre?'

She steps forwards and trips again. Her hands land on sharp shards. Livvy ignores the pain.

'Mommy! Mommy!'

'Andre?' Livvy rises quickly, but she doesn't hear the child anymore. Instead, there's the crunch of shoes on rubble-covered pavement. Then the sound of a car door as it clicks shut. An engine revs.

Livvy lurches forwards and slaps her hand onto soft, stretched skin.

It yields and flattens, *splat!*

A moment's horror, then Livvy realises she's at the sports hall door. A shrivelled rag from one of the doorway balloons is in her grasp. How was it still intact? A balloon survived this when her own eyes couldn't?

Livvy pulls at the door. It's stuck. She tugs and there's a muffled noise, like an explosion under water, then the screams of the children hit her in a wave of shrieks.

A peculiar smell prickles the inside of Livvy's nostrils. That's when the realisation hits her: there's no scent of burning, no sense of fire at all. She can't hear it crackling or feel the heat fluctuating from the flames. That's good, surely. She begins walking forwards, crouching when anyone collides with her leg, trying to discern the sounds of the child, the features of its head.

'Andre? Marcie?'

'Mommy!' Several children yell back, desperate to connect a mother to a voice, *'Mommy!'*

Livvy's head swivels, trying to get the maximum information from her surroundings.

Panic rises as she struggles to discern her own babies. Her ears work at least, but she has never had to locate her children in darkness, noise and mayhem before. She feels like a ewe trapped in a slaughterhouse, trying to detect her own lambs with terror all around her.

'Andre? Marcie? Is that you?'

Arms surround her knees. Livvy bends and tries to pick up the small body that has locked itself onto her legs. 'Andre? Marcie?' The tiny limbs are wrapped securely. Livvy's hand rises, feels the longer strands, then realises as the child speaks that it must be her daughter.

'Mommy! Mommy!'

'Is that you, Marcie?'

'Mommy, why is it so dark? I can't see you!'

'Oh my God, Marcie, thank God, thank God!'

Livvy lifts Marcie up to her chest and holds her so snugly that the little girl can hardly breathe, but Marcie doesn't mind. She clings on equally tightly, burrowing herself into her mother's neck as if she wants to be inside her skin. Livvy tries to inhale her daughter's familiar scent but there is only that peculiar odour clinging to Marcie's clothes.

'Oh, Marcie my darling! But where's Andre?'

The screams subside as parents locate and claim children, but still there are high, desperate calls, 'Mommy!'

'Andre?' Livvy yells, swivelling, waiting for the response, but that cry she heard before is gone.

'Here lady,' a man's muffled voice appears beside her. It sounds as if he is wearing a mask. 'Here is your son.'

The man passes a wilted body onto Livvy's free shoulder. She sags a little under the weight of two children, but clutches them tight. 'Oh God, Oh God, is he – ? Is he – ? Is he alright?'

Livvy's arm flails up the child's torso, trying to find a response. As she reaches his head, she flattens his soft hair, still upright, though thick with dust, and runs her fingers over his face. It's dry and soft; there's no sense of the wetness nor scent of blood. Livvy kisses his cheek in relief, but notes that it smells strange. The effects of the bomb, she supposes.

'He's unconscious, ma'am.' Another man has joined them; his drawl has a more familiar accent. It's easier to hear, though still muffled. A better mask, perhaps.

'Aren't you blind?' Livvy asks. 'Can you see?' She wheels desperately and staggers over something soft. A body, maybe.

'I can see, ma'am.' The man grabs her arms, steadying her and supporting the children. Marcie whimpers and clutches even closer onto the skin around Livvy's neck. The child's fingers leave a fringe of imprints that will be there for days.

Andre is still limp, he feels lifeless. Livvy's legs are beginning to tremble and shake.

'Let me help you, ma'am.' The man tries to lift the children from her, but she holds on tenaciously, her arms fastened around the little bodies.

'No!' Livvy snaps, 'No, don't take them.'

There's a click of a radio, a mumbled interchange Livvy can't make out. Then the man's hand simply steers Livvy's arm instead of grabbing it. 'Keep calm, ma'am, come and sit down,' he levers her onto a plastic seat. 'Wait here. I'll get a medic.'

The man leaves and Livvy feels a brief sense of relief. But then she realises that she is alone amidst the suffocating cries of Hell.

Livvy waits, shivering. She struggles to control the urge to run, scream, shout and weep. Bending low, she shelters the two small heads under her own, hands covering their ears. She does not want to alarm Marcie, who is very much awake, nor disturb Andre, even if he is scarily silent.

She does not feel as though her son is dead. Though he is mute and unresponsive, she believes she would know if the worst had happened. Twice she thinks she hears him snuffling, but it is difficult to be sure as Marcie has begun weeping.

'Please put the lights on, mommy, I'm frightened. Please mommy, *please*!'

Livvy shifts her position, certain that she can feel the flaccid warmth of a body lying on the floor alongside.

She keeps her feet immobile beneath her and tries not to listen to the dreadful sounds. To distract the children, Livvy rocks them gently, tilting forwards, murmuring, 'The lights are broken, angel, but someone will sort them. Remember the see-saw song?'

Livvy murmurs *'see-saw, see-saw'*, over and over, unable to recall the rest of the words, but it works, Marcie's fretfulness subsides.

As Livvy breathes through her nightmare, the minutes are as painfully oppressive as they were during childbirth. She remembers the lessons learned then, and starts counting her inhalations, consoling herself that at least she has found her children, and they are alive.

At last, a medic arrives. He ascertains that the toddlers are well, only dazed, and informs Livvy that the blindness will pass. Others on the periphery of the base are already recovering from the temporary effects of the gas.

Livvy is travelling slowly in the back of an armoured car, which noses reluctantly over the sleeping policemen, when the darkness begins to shift and change into a foggy patchwork of lights. Her eyes seep as an apparition of outlines appears through the gloom. It reminds Livvy of their last family holiday, driving through a muzzy, wet fret in a seaside resort. She hugs her children tightly, looking down upon their resting heads with relieved appreciation.

Then she blinks at the darker hair of the child on her right.

Livvy raises her hand to wipe her eyes, rubs harshly,

and looks down again.

Livvy's movements disturb the little boy. He pushes himself upwards, still leaning his weight on her, and rubs his eyes too. But as he tilts his unknown face to stare at her, his expression mirrors hers. Their faces break into horror and confusion.

Livvy starts to scream.

She awakens at home, laid out on her own sofa, her right arm sore and bandaged.

Cory is by her side. Behind him the television blares out the News Channel, again displaying the red band. Though Livvy's eyesight has not fully returned, her sense of hearing is still acute. When she hears a thump from upstairs, it seems unusually loud. She tries to sit up, but Cory eases her backwards.

'You've been sedated, honey.' He says gently, kneeling alongside her.

Livvy peers blearily past him, looking at her house. The effect of the drugs and the apricot walls combine to give the room a fuzzy, delusional appearance, but everything is in its place, apparently normal. Even the noises from upstairs are the ordinary sounds of children playing. Livvy relaxes. For a moment she feels like it's all been a dream.

'I had this most awful nightmare,' she begins, smiling at Cory and ready to make fun of her own absurdity.

'Like I said, you've been sedated. The doctor said it's bound to have some strange effects.'

'But it was a really bad one. I dreamed that Andre was replaced by a completely different child.'

Cory's eyes flicker away and his hand scratches the corner of his mouth.

Livvy's expression changes instantly: 'No! No! It can't be!'

She tries to get up, but Cory holds her down. Her hands flail at him in vain. When he tries to stop her by gripping her sore arm, she screams. In an instant, an orderly comes running in from the kitchen. Livvy's head twists round in surprise. She hadn't known anyone was there.

Between the two men, her bandage is swiftly unwrapped and an ampule attached to the tube which juts from her skin just above her wrist. Within seconds a numbing warmth runs up her arm and suffuses her body. Every effort becomes utterly exhausting and Livvy's head is eddying. In the end it is easy for Cory to press her backwards, and he nods the orderly back to the kitchen.

Livvy sags into her sofa, wretched and despondent. The effects of Cory's behaviour and the medication make her brain imagine a great separation between herself and her husband. She fixes her gaze upon his upright figure, squinting at him as though he were a distant mountain, and starts flinging anxious sentences in his direction.

'Is he upstairs now?'

'Yes.'

'Dear God! What if he does something to Marcie?'

'He's tiny! A small child!'

'But still!'

'Livvy! The poor little chap's only just come round. He was crying, but we've given him a slight sedative too.'

Livvy glares at Cory as harshly as she can. 'A sedative? You said "he's tiny. A small child".'

His voice slows, 'Slight sedative,' he repeats, 'Not as strong as yours, and you're okay. And there's an army nurse sitting with them.'

'But what did Marcie say? How's my baby girl?'

The tears run like watered blood down Livvy's cheeks. Cory hopes it is the last traces of the substance in the gas; it is dreadfully unnerving.

'Once she got her sight back, she was surprisingly perky. You know Marcie, likes to be in there, joining in. Obviously she's a bit bemused, but she's gamely going round, showing him the toys.' Another thump comes from upstairs. 'That'll be an extra box they're opening.'

'This can't be real, it really can't!'

Another wave of nausea. Livvy covers her mouth with her hands and sobs into them.

'I'm sorry, but it is, darling. They've swapped our sons.'

Cory comes forward and crouches down. He stretches a tentative arm towards Livvy, but she turns away, hiding her face in her hands. Cory coughs and stands up.

'It's quite an honour in a way.'

'What?' She swivels back to confront him, 'How?'

'They wouldn't give their child to us if they didn't think we would look after him.'

'But who's looking after *our* child? The sort of monster who volunteers to give his own son away?'

Livvy's heart aches as she thinks of her boy. The pain grips hard and taut.

'Well, I'm not sure how voluntary it was, but I know that in their country they have a different emphasis on things. They value honour and sacrifice.'

'So do we: in adults! But oh my God, Cory! You can't sacrifice a child. My poor son!' Her whole being caves into the agony. She wraps her arms around her empty body.

'Our son, Livvy. He's mine too.'

'Our only son, why did they take him? Why would they take *our* child?'

'Practical reasons, bluntly. He's the same age, almost, as the child we have upstairs. He is also the son of a high-ranking officer tipped to be a ruler in their new regime. The boys are our guarantee that we will not harm each other.'

Livvy waves a hand at him dismissively, 'Oh don't! It's like something medieval for God's sake! Utterly ridiculous in this day and age! That's what we have diplomats for!'

'Diplomats are not leaders, Livvy.'

'He's a baby human shield, that's what he is!'

Livvy's breath quickens as it had in labour. She holds onto her abdomen as if she hopes to return her child there.

'And,' she pants, glaring at Cory with that same narrowed accusatory stare, 'Whoever is in charge of things on our side, well, they'll just dismiss him as collateral damage or something!'

'It's not like that, Liv!'

'But it is already! People's children are dying all the time. You write those awful letters to the poor parents with that same phrase "Sorry for your loss"! You let *their* sons die and you call it friendly fire!'

Finally, Cory's military demeanour is shaken. He drops to his knees, clutching at her hands, desperately trying to hold them.

'Oh God, Livvy, stop, please stop – please!'

Cory's face crumples, his grip nips her fingers, 'No one would knowingly slaughter their own son, that's why they chose us.'

'But they've made a mistake!' Livvy blurts triumphantly, suddenly hopeful. 'You're not that high up – you're not responsible – '

'No, well, I'm not now. Not yet.' He squints in the direction of the kitchen, releases Livvy and leans a fist against his temple. 'But you know, they don't advertise posts for the person whose finger will actually touch the button.'

Rising to his feet, Cory automatically brushes away the carpet fluff from his trousers, glancing once more towards the empty doorway.

'Someone somewhere must think I'm heading for the top. It's a compliment, really.'

That moment, Livvy hates him. She looks up through her running eyes, her hands rubbing against her sticky, stained cheeks, and wishes she were blind again, so that she did not have to see the way his mouth tightened in anticipation of power.

'It's kidnapping!'

'It's supposed to be an exchange – like they do in schools, a cultural exchange – at least that's how our government are promoting it to the World's media.'

Libby stares at him. 'But they're doing everything they can to get him back, surely? Is it the SEALs or the SAS?'

There is silence. Seconds of un-reverberating air. The atmosphere thickens with each moment that he will not look at her.

'You bastard! You cruel bastard!'

With supreme efforts, Livvy rises upwards and began to thump, push and shove.

But Cory simply catches her fists.

Enraged, she pulls away from him, shouting with drugged fury, just as she had done in the throes of their children's birth. The orderly rushes in again but Cory shakes his head and the man gratefully retreats.

'Get our baby back!' Livvy pleads, still trying to tug her arms free, 'Send the men to get him! Send in the troops!'

'And risk him dead?' Cory retorts, pushing Livvy away so furiously that she slumps into the sofa. 'The powers that be are relieved, truth be told. They regretted the bomb the minute that idiot pressed the bloody button. Nobody intended him to do it, it was supposed to be a threat, but he was too stupid a puppet to understand innuendo.'

'Too easily words of war become acts of war.' Livvy quotes, dully.

'It's difficult to choose a figurehead with the right level of intelligence,' Cory murmurs, 'too clever and they start to question the advisors, too stupid and they blindly follow them.'

Livvy shakes her head, stunned. Her husband is a stranger to her.

'If it's any consolation, the other mother's as distraught as you.'

Instantly Livvy is in communion with her unknown co-mother. This morning they were adversaries.

'We'll be meeting with them regularly over the course of the year. We'll have residential diplomatic visits. The children will each know who's their Mom.'

'Oh God! I don't know if that's better or worse,' Livvy starts weeping again. 'They'll be like little lost boys. It's so cruel!'

'It will save Andre's life, and not only his, but potentially millions across the globe. If the retaliation had continued, anybody not directly killed by the blasts would have been poisoned slowly over time. As would whole generations ever after.'

Livvy shudders, quietened, 'But it's inhuman.'

'No, it's not, it's part of civilisation, a practice that's been accepted for centuries, sending children to live with others to give them the chance of a better life. A form of adoption, that's all. One of your favourite authors – Jane Austen – her brother got sent away, remember? He was ultimately in a position to help his entire family.'

'But Andre's so young,' Livvy pictures her small son, couched in her arms that morning, miserable because of the fire engine. She begins sobbing again. 'It'll be *so* hard for him! Who's going to hold him when he wakes in the night, scared, and he's all alone? I can't bear to think of him crying in the dark on his own!'

Her head drops. Livvy's tears run red as blood. Cory hates them.

'Oh Livvy for God's sake, we're supposed to be Christians, right? Children are a gift to the world, a blessing. Our child is still alive. Be grateful for their mercy. They could have killed us all, easily, by using a different gas.' Cory clears his throat. 'And *we* killed first, remember?'

He takes his wife's hand and this time she doesn't remove it.

The lines between his eyes soften. 'They gave us this chance to save him, and lots of other children too. It's a gift of life, to us, and the whole world. I know he's had to go away, but – '

'But why shouldn't they give him back?'

'Livvy, think of the story of Samuel. Remember how you told me how his mom couldn't have children? You read it to me when we were waiting for the IVF injections that day?'

'Yes.' Livvy stares at Cory with venom: she already knows where he's going with this.

'You said if you prayed like Samuel's mom, you too would be blessed, didn't you?' Cory meets her gaze and keeps it, forcing the admission.

Livvy closes her eyes. The word drops soft and slow as spittle from her lips. 'Yes.'

'And what happened to Samuel's mom?'

She opens her eyes again, mouths, 'You bastard.'

His gaze points towards the kitchen.

Livvy's head drops. 'She had to give him away.'

'Yes, she did, she gave him away and she was blessed with more children.'

'I don't want to be blessed with more!'

'No, and I'm not suggesting it, because we have Marcie and this other little boy – my point is …'

'I know what your point is,' Livvy says coldly, raising her gaze with as much precision and hostility as though she were targeting the trajectory of a massive gun.

In the silence, their eyes challenge like enemies.

Cory looks away first.

Suddenly loud into the quiet expanse, the television speaks: 'And back to today's main story. In an innovative, diplomatic move that commentators are already praising …'

Cory jumps up and flicks off the television at the switch. 'I'm off to check on the kids.'

His ordinary statement is like a detonation. Livvy flares up, trying to get up after him, but the effect of the drugs sends her legs collapsing to the floor. She shouts after Cory, clawing the carpet, but he is gone.

Defeated, Livvy gives in and sobs into the rug whose thick, banded swirls Andre used to pretend were roads.

Livvy lays her head to the pile like Andre did. Following the patterns with her fingers, she at last locates the source of her son's despair that morning, the lost toy jammed underneath the back of the sofa.

Livvy succeeds in retrieving it, but as she picks up the tiny fire engine, she catches the red button on the top and the siren goes off in her hand.

Slumped on the floor, Livvy hugs Andre's toy tight to her chest. She sits and cries, pressing the red button continuously.

A miniature blue light sends sweeping flashes across her face. The siren's high whine wails in circles round her head.

Polishing the Galaxies

MICHAEL YATES

A funny thing has happened to me. When I say *funny* I don't mean laughable. I mean very strange. But serious. I *do* mean *serious*. And I've been suffering like this for some years now, give or take. Though it's not the end of the world, of course.

I want to tell you first of all what an ordinary sort of man I am. *Was*. Am *still* in many ways. I'm married. I have a baby son. *Had* a baby son. There. You're confused, I can tell. I'd better start at the beginning.

I'm an accountant. I love being an accountant. One reason is the figures in their neat columns. In and out, Revenue and Expenses. Some time back, it became *more* than neatness. I'd been reading things about mathematics – mostly on Wikipedia – and somehow I suddenly discovered the beauty of each number, what each number means in the way of proportion, relationships to other qualities, part of a wholesome whole. I can't quite describe it. A universal jigsaw if you like, where I can match the colour and shape of each number in a beautiful pattern.

It's what God must see when He's polishing His galaxies, or whatever He does. If there *is* a God. As Einstein said, mathematics is the poetry of logical ideas. I felt good when I read that. I'd never thought of myself as a poet before.

I married Heather five years ago. She was really my first proper girlfriend. I guess I'm a shy person. But we seemed well suited. Heather was lots of fun. She was in PR and she already knew some really important people in showbiz and politics. We seemed made for each other – forever. Well, *forever* barring accident or happenstance, of course. I guess happenstance is the best way to describe the way it's turned out.

About three years ago, I started getting headaches. I was working in those days for Klein, Mallory & Knickerbokker, one of the top seven firms. And I was working very hard. Late nights at the computer. Problems with some of my clients.

Lochinvar, the online nutrition and beauty retailer, had suffered a haemorrhage in its share price and some of the people there were blaming me. God knows why. If there *is* a God, as I said. And Normandy, the private equity company, had made a disastrous mistake in their takeover bid for Bournemouth Insurance, but I'd warned them explicitly not to go for it at that time. So, I wasn't going to take the blame for *that*.

One night, it was about 3am when I finally climbed into bed with Heather and I accidentally woke her up. I told her about the headaches and she said: 'Take some Paracetamol.' And I did. But I didn't sleep much, so I got up around five and went for a drive.

Did you notice that? Five and drive. They rhyme. I hadn't intended that, but they do. It's not just numbers that have their balance and their beauty. It's words too. Just about everything really – if you can see it, if you acknowledge it. Harmony everywhere.

So I went driving in my BMW. Not far, just round the block. Just the places I know that make me feel comfortable. I noticed on the way how some of the semis had put up white stone cladding over their brickwork. I know some people were complaining about how these houses stuck out badly against the *redbrickness* of the neighbourhood. But to me they were just another sort of matching: white with red, all part of the spectrum, after all. Why couldn't people see that?

And a cat ran across the road. And I hit it. No way not to. I got out of the car and ran over to see how bad it was – all bloody and caved in. I'm afraid it was dead. I picked it up by the tail and took it over to the bus stop and dropped it in the rubbish bin. And I got back in the car.

And that was quite sad. I could *see* it was sad. Sad for the cat. Sad for me really because I'd done something quite unintended. I mean, I never had anything against the cat. I quite like cats. But at the same time, I could see that for some creatures in this world, say mice or canaries, one less cat was quite a good thing. So it all evens out within the workings of the universe.

Take malaria for instance. I hear there's a miracle drug been invented to combat malaria and it will save maybe millions of lives in tropical countries. But is that really such a good thing? I also keep reading that the world is being ruined by overpopulation and forests of the Amazon are being cleared for mining and farming and other things so maybe having more people is not really a good thing after all. Not *totally* good anyway. It's all a matter of checks and balances in this amazing universe that's all run by beautiful numbers. We have to remember that and have a sense of perspective.

Paul Dirac, the English physicist who is buried in Florida, said God used beautiful mathematics in creating the world. Though I don't quite know what Dirac meant by God, as you must realise by now.

Then Lochinvar went to another firm (I think it was Morgan Masters). And Normandy went into liquidation and the chairman was prosecuted for skimming millions off the revenue and a lot of people asked why *I'd* not realised this. But what can you say? He'd worked hard for the firm and made millions for people in the days when things were going well. Maybe he should have been paid more. Like I said, his only mistake really was buying Bournemouth Insurance when he did.

Then Klein, Mallory & Knickerbokker let me go. I mean *let me go*. Just like that. It was a hole in our income but I didn't want to tell Heather. I mean some people — the kind of people who can't see the natural balance of things — might have thought it really was the end of the world. But I saw it as an opportunity to develop myself.

And then Heather said she was pregnant. And I was overjoyed. But she wanted to quit Main Media, the outfit she worked for, and be a mum for a while. And who can blame her? It's a wonderful thing bringing new life into the world, even if it *is* leading to overpopulation, as I remarked a little earlier. And I said: Yes. Okay. I was sure we could keep our heads above water. Even without Klein, Mallory & Knickerbokker, though I still hadn't told her that. Yes. Fine.

My headaches weren't getting any better. In fact, I think they were worse, though I wasn't quite sure. I mean, the Paracetamol *did* make a difference, so I thought: Well, I'll be okay, whatever. But I also had some pains in my fingers, maybe arthritis, so I'd started on Ibuprofen as well because I read it was okay to take more tablets if you alternated between the two of them. It was statistically safe. Actually, more than that: very even-handed, emotionally very satisfying.

Then I got into trouble with Gaspol, the Polish oil and gas company which was starting to grow because of the war in Ukraine. Gaspol was the one client that kept me on through personal loyalty.

The CEO of Gaspol UK phoned me from a phone box. I said: 'I didn't know there were such things as phone boxes anymore, what with mobile phones and all.' He laughed. He said phone boxes were very useful. He said he'd like to meet with me, but it had to be private, no need to put it in my diary. Just come to Waterloo Bridge and bring some breadcrumbs. He said: 'We can feed the birds there. Lots of people do it.'

So I did. And I took a large fork out of the kitchen, about a foot long, stainless steel with a wooden handle, and I rubbed it down with a wet rag and I put it into the M&S plastic bag that I was using for my breadcrumbs. Don't ask me why I took the fork. I suppose I was a bit suspicious of all this sudden secrecy. I just thought I might need it somehow.

And he was waiting for me, a small, chubby man, all smiles. And he said there was a problem with a shares issue and what he needed was some *creative accounting*. 'I know you're the man to do it,' he said, 'because I know you worked for Normandy. In fact, that's why we kept you on.'

'Oh,' I said.

And he talked me through it. But I didn't really listen. We weren't standing on the bridge itself, we were by the side of the river, throwing the breadcrumbs and leaning against a very large bridge support (I think it's called a stanchion) so people passing by couldn't really see us. I was quite upset. I didn't like the idea that he thought I was some kind of crook. And my headache had got quite a bit worse.

And when I'd thrown in all my breadcrumbs, I took out the kitchen fork and stuck it in his throat. He looked quite surprised. And then he fell in the river. It wasn't much of a splash and no-one came running to see what had happened. I walked back to the road and caught a bus and, when I got to Kings Cross station, I dropped my gloves in a rubbish bin. And that reminded me of the cat. And I thought: it's a different kind of rhyme to a *word* rhyme, but it's a rhyme all the same. Happenings can rhyme just as much as words. It was the natural balance of things.

Afterwards, I admit I felt a little bad about what I'd done. But then I remembered what Shakuntala Devi, who was known as The Human Computer, said: Everything around you is numbers. I suppose she meant we all have to make them add up, come what may.

We called the baby Adam because he was our first. And things were really fine for a time. But I failed to get any new accounts. I think the publicity about Gaspol probably hurt me: the death of the chubby man, whose name I can never remember now, and the discovery that he'd been syphoning off millions just like the Normandy man. The police seemed to think he'd committed suicide and I was quite annoyed by this. What do we pay our taxes for if the police are so sloppy?

Well, I tried hard to get new clients, but I didn't make any progress. And I couldn't possibly tell Heather. I didn't want to spoil things because Adam was coming along so well and we were all so happy. But one day I thought: I can't go on like this. I realised it was best if I *never* had to tell her. But then what would happen to Adam, if his mummy died? No, that was just too cruel. I knew I'd have to kill him as well.

And that made sense in the scheme of things. Millions of babies are born every year, and many of them, mainly in poorer countries, soon die. Here was a chance to make things more equitable in one of the developed nations. The way I decided to kill Heather was to crush 50 of my Paracetamol and put them in her coffee flask when she went out with her friends in the Wandsworth Women's Walking Club. And while she was away, I put the rest of them in Adam's bottle and he guzzled away quite happily.

In that moment, I remembered something Bertrand Russell had said: In the modern world the stupid are cocksure while the intelligent are full of doubt. But how could that be? I *certainly* wasn't full of doubt.

Then I sat down to read the *Daily Telegraph*. I was sure the police would catch up with me this time and I was quite prepared to admit killing the chubby man and even the cat if it made things easier for them. Then I got to reading an article about Charles Whitman, an American I'd never previously heard of, who'd murdered his wife and mother, then climbed a water tower at the University of Texas and killed eleven people with his hunting rifle. He was shot dead by police, of course. And then they found a confession at his home saying: 'Lately I have been a victim of many unusual and irrational thoughts.' He requested an autopsy to be performed on him. And when the doctors cut him open, guess what? They found a large tumour in his brain and all was explained.

Well, I thought, I'm quite happy to have them do the same to me. That way I may be able to make a considerable contribution to medical science. Wouldn't that be wonderful?

Which just goes to show there really *is* a perfect balance to the Universe, God or no God. And because this is true, things will just go on for ever, balancing out, intermingling and interacting. So there will never, never be an end to this wonderful world, Armageddon or Apocalypse, or whatever you want to call it.

QED.

The End

RUTH CHEESBROUGH

Sometimes the end of the world is sudden and brutal: the unanticipated break up, or that unexpected death. Sometimes the end of the world is so slow and gradual that you don't even notice it: your beloved mum slipping further and further into dementia, until you can't even say on which day she just wasn't your mum anymore. It wasn't until today, when I peeled my VR headset off after another eight-hour shift, that I realised the world had already ended. Oh, there had been clues – rampant climate change, energy shortages, overpopulation, the new laws, the metaverse – and I hadn't missed them, but it took seeing my face in the mirror, lined and tired, with great red marks where my headset had been, to make me notice. My face was an older echo of my pandemic face, bruised from PPE and broken from dying. But do you know what? If I could, I'd turn the world back to 2020 in a heartbeat.

I don't have patients anymore. Well, I do, I just see them in virtual reality. I'm not allowed to operate on them directly, instead, I clock into my metaverse hospital. I try to imagine them, real people, sealed into their surgical caskets, but it's not easy. It's supposed to be better this way, safe from the risk of infection now that we don't have effective antibiotics, and safe from the surgeon's error with all the AI checks. Soon it will all be done by AI, and I'll be out of a job. I'm past caring.

In 2020, after a shift, I'd go home to my boyfriend and my dog. Whenever it was light enough and we had the energy, we'd take Barney up on the moors and walk until our muscles had stretched and our heads had calmed. Other times, we'd sit in companionable silence, losing ourselves in books. Barney would lie against me, partly on me, a great 40kg lap dog. His warmth soaked into me like a soothing potion, and for a little while, the world would be just right. That's how I got through the pandemic: with Barney, with Fran, with books, and the moors. Now they're all gone.

Fran was the first to go. It was one of those sudden, brutal endings. I should have seen it coming but I'd have sworn we'd be together forever. I blamed it on biology, that sudden urge to have a child. I don't know what came over me: one month I was a career focused doctor, the next, my period arrived like a gush of despair from my barren womb. I was desperate to have a child because suddenly my empty womb was unbearable. It was as simple as that. I knew better than to try and explain to Fran that every month, despite his careful monitoring of our contraception, I'd hoped I'd miraculously fall pregnant. And if I was being absolutely, embarrassingly honest, a tiny part of me, expected to.

Fran didn't understand. He thought that I was insane for wanting to bring a child into this world. To be fair, he had recognised where the world was heading long before I did, but even if I'd realised the full extent of the metaverse back then it wouldn't have made a difference: I just wanted something perfect to hold on to. He was furious that so much of his work had to be done digitally, and if any of his clients asked him to design anything for the metaverse, he angrily refused. Fran just seemed to get angrier and angrier. He started to remind me of all those eco-fascists and other extremists you saw on the news, the way he ranted on about all his research, his blue eyes blazing. Climate change wouldn't be so bad in Vermont, he would say, it's one of the least populated US states, so we could go there and live how people should live, off grid, away from the metaverse. I suppose I should have listened to him, but the metaverse still wasn't real to me then. I knew all about it, but my days were rooted in reality, in life and death at the hospital, with real people with real problems. I knew some people spent hours in the metaverse, but I didn't know any of those people.

Every evening when I got home, Fran went on about Vermont, about how we'd live off grid, in the real world. About how he knew somebody who knew somebody who'd sort the paperwork. It was as if rules and laws were to be just disregarded. He claimed that there was still plenty of space in Vermont and nobody would resent our arrival. Even in my exhausted state I questioned that and was told that if the worst came to the worst, we'd just travel up to Canada.

This went on for weeks and weeks and weeks. Worst was in the mornings after my night shifts when I was truly desperate to sleep. Barney became my only consolation. Of course, I'd asked about what we'd do with Barney and Fran told me, matter-of-factly, that an odd couple down the road would be happy to have him. I threw a book at him then. I'm ashamed to admit it.

Eventually, one September Saturday, Fran told me that we'd be leaving on the Monday. I shouldn't have been shocked, but I was.

I didn't go. Fran and I said goodbye like strangers, but then, as he reached the door, he turned, and somehow, just for a moment, the old Fran was standing there. He promised he'd write, that I could join him later. Shortly afterwards, post was restricted in order to save resources, and personal communication was only allowed through email. Fran's principles were obviously more important to him than contacting me. I never heard from him again.

After Fran left, it was just me and Barney. There was nobody else to turn to. The way Barney gazed at me with his beautiful brown eyes and laid against me at night, his warmth seeping into me, brought me some comfort and eased the loneliness. All the same, I woke every morning with an empty anxious feeling knowing that time was running out. Big dogs like Barney usually only live ten years or so. I watched the grey hairs multiplying around his muzzle and stiffness creeping into his joints. It wasn't long before I lost Barney too, silently, in his sleep one night.

I don't know if the moors are still there. I heard they were building on them, as crazy as it sounds. I can't even go and look, only the remaining real-world workers are allowed out without restrictions. Apparently, the country has got too crowded.

I still have my books. Some of them: the ones I could cram into my tiny flat. I tried to pick a variety and my favourites. I run my fingers over their spines sometimes. I don't know what I'm hoping for, maybe transportation into another world, but it never happens. I don't seem to have the concentration for reading anymore. And there's no way I'm going to buy books in the metaverse, the way you're supposed to, and keep my eyes glued to a screen all my waking hours. Printing physical books is a waste of precious resources and therefore illegal, so now we have crap churned out by computers instead.

After gulping down some water, I get on the treadmill out of habit. I get a decent discount off my health insurance if I clock up at least five kilometres a day, but I don't do it because of that. There's nothing I want to spend money on anymore. I do it because exercise is the only thing that gets rid of the anger.

'Fuck the metaverse, fuck surgical caskets, fuck climate change,' I huff, 'Fuck my job, fuck my life. Fuck Fran for leaving me here alone.'

I can't take any more. I really can't take any more. Today I realised that the world has already ended.

I'm not ready to end with it.

That last thought surprises me. I thought I was. There is nothing to live for. I think of Fran in Vermont, wonder if he's out there camped out beside a river, or hiding in a forest. I know he won't be in a house, unless he's got a tiny shack hidden away somewhere. US laws are no less strict than ours. I wonder if he's even still alive.

I step off the treadmill after only about two and a half kilometres. Today it's not making me any less angry, it just seems utterly pointless. My hiking boots are at the back of the wardrobe, coated with a thin layer of mud that's been there maybe five years. There's my rucksack too and I drag it out, begin to throw things in carelessly, and then with a manic sense of purpose. I find waterproofs, thick socks, things I haven't needed for a long time. Food comes in sachets now, all made in a lab. I throw some in.

I pull my phone out of my pocket. It's lit up with all the notifications that were blocked when I was working. I swipe them away: work stuff, adverts and some large and lurid penis. Dick pics were bad enough before the metaverse but now there are infinite VR versions. I leave the phone on the table. I'm almost out the door before I go back, find my doctor's bag and stuff some of the contents into my bulging rucksack.

Outside, it's dark and there's a gentle summer breeze blowing. It reminds me of those long-ago student summer nights, when I'd step out of a night club feeling like the night was just beginning, and I could stay awake forever. I'd drag my friends out to the edge of the city to watch the sunrise. There are no seasons in the metaverse, just a weird mishmash of mainly spring and summer, like a book nobody bothered to edit. There are sunrises and sunsets all over the place too. It's easy to lose track of reality.

I pull my hood up and between that and the black fabric face mask, there's not much of my face showing but I still feel exposed. There are no streetlights, no security lights to light up as I creep by either. They were outlawed years ago. Otherwise, this street is much the same as it's always been, huddled back to backs, each one now divided into two flats, stepping away down the hillside. They'll be knocked down one day and rebuilt into more flats if things go on long enough. I take the little dirt path on the left, picking my way along, stepping carefully over fallen stones from a forgotten wall, bits of vegetation and long, long discarded rubbish. On the next road there's a lone car transporting someone to or from a real-world job, and a couple of robots out on deliveries. Staying as far into the pavement as I can, I creep up the hill. Light seeps grudgingly out from curtained windows and brazenly out of lit up stairwells, as if there is no energy crisis at all. Tall blocks of flats stand where houses used to be.

I know my way but it's confusing how everything's changed in such a short time and the darkness is disconcerting. I used to love to walk the fields, not seeing where my feet would land, owls hooting all around me. Here it feels like there's danger around every corner. I find a path where I think the path should be, but it just leads me into a maze of further paths going round and round a housing estate and back to where I started. The old paths must still be here somewhere, laid down in stone by workers in a different world, but I expect they're buried now, lying beneath all these buildings that have sprung up, and will fall down one day. They'll still be here when we're dead and gone. I follow the road, on and on, following the red lights of the odd car, the flashing lights of the robots, on into the darkness. There is hardly any noise in a world that's dead already.

Eventually, I cross the final road, my heart lurching with the thought that I'm almost there. I should be able to see the moors stretching up before me but it's too dark and I'm all hemmed in by buildings. The track that I'm looking for is gone. I won't panic. I try a little path between the buildings. It's like a labyrinth, tall blocks with doors here and there, marked with letters and numbers. I try to keep heading west but there's nothing to guide me. I can't see the moon. There's nothing but the towering buildings disappearing up into the blackness. The sky is splattered with stars, but I don't know how to use them as guides. I walk round in circles for what feels like hours. My rucksack is getting heavier with every step, there's a dull ache in the small of my back and my shoulders are smarting under the straps. I think of giving up, but I can't go back. There is nobody to help me. I stumble on until I'm almost knocked over by a robot. It disappears around the corner before I've even properly registered what happened. I look for a path that's sloping up. I find one and suddenly know I'm going the right way.

I keep expecting the buildings to peter out, keep expecting to find myself on the old track, the fields of sheep on either side of me. I can't believe that the old track is gone, but it must be because I'm still climbing upwards and there's just buildings and tarmac. It's hard to judge how far I've come. I wonder if I've passed the ruined farmhouse where make-believe toffs, in tweed jackets and flat caps, used to shoot clay pigeons. It must be gone, replaced by these hastily erected buildings. I feel the ground flattening out and realise I should be on the moor but under my feet there is tarmac. I keep walking until all there is ahead of me is darkness. The path gives way to rough grass strewn with rubble and underneath I know there's that beloved black peat, scattered in places with silvery sand. I step further and further away from the buildings, slowly, carefully. The ground is uneven and the darkness is absolute. I reach a big rock and sit down on its smooth surface, pulling a blanket from my rucksack to wrap around me. I've been walking for hours and I'm exhausted. It's madness to walk the moors, what's left of the moors, in this darkness.

I wake cold and aching under a lightening sky. I sit up and realise I'm right on the edge of the clough, the one called Great Scar that runs right down to the reservoir. If I'd have stepped off the other side of this rock I'd have fallen to my death.

'Thank you,' I whisper, but I'm not sure who I'm thanking.

My fingers feel for the yin yang sign that's been carved into the rock. It's been there as long as I remember.

The sun is slowly rising. I watch as it begins to glint off the windows of the new buildings on the other side of the valley. I take out a pouch of food, it's supposed to be porridge flavour, and I swallow the beige congealing contents, wash them down with water, and I'm on my way. I must be cracking up because I see Barney trotting just ahead of me, tail up, nose down, sniffing out the route. I thought I'd held the image of Barney securely in my head, backed up by all those photos I'd taken, but his tail looks fluffier than I remember. Barney runs ahead of me, going just the way I want to go. He trots along the path that runs right on the edge of the clough, just as it's always done. Bracken and heather spring up to brush my ankles and I bend to pick a perfect purple sprig, clutching it in my hand like a charm.

The sky is pink now, a bit like a washed-out version of the heather, and birds are singing. Those little ones I don't know the names of. On and on we go across the moor, climbing up past the cairns, Barney's feathered tail waving before me like a flag. The reservoir is still here, its blue stretches out to a shore on the other side littered with buildings. An endless city that stretches as far as the eye can see. But up here, there is still moor. When the first giggling grouse rushes up out of the heather, Barney turns and faces me. He's never bothered grouse. At the summit, we turn and head into the heart of the moor.

As I slip along the old paths, balancing on the ridges to keep my feet dry, I realise I'm smiling. Barney comes back to walk beside me, and I rub his head. It's softer than I remember. Everything is the same and yet everything is different. The feeling of peat under my feet makes me feel like I could walk forever: it caresses my feet as they touch down and throws them up for another step. If I step into a boggy part, feel the suck as the ground closes around my foot, I know there is no malice in it. For me the moors have always been home.

Stones are everywhere, reminding me of the quarries long past, back when the moors were teeming with workers. I prefer it like this, just me and Barney and a curlew crying somewhere overhead. It's not barren though, I don't know why people use that word. Barren is my empty womb, still mocking me with its perfect twenty-eight day cycles and ovulation pain. The moor is teeming with life if you know where to look.

I follow Barney and the path as it winds around two cloughs and on and up to the weird stone cairns. I've never known who built them or why. There's one shaped like a question mark, and another two that maybe spell out the number forty-two, if viewed from above. Or maybe that's just wishful thinking. Someone once told me that back in the '90s there were illegal raves up here. It's hard to imagine the cars and vans travelling along the long lonely twisting road and their occupants stumbling across the dark moors, some carrying sound systems, most high on drugs. I think maybe the cairns here were built by the ravers, in the mornings after, coming down from their highs.

The sun has been steadily climbing the sky as I've walked and it's getting too hot already. Barney's tongue is hanging out; he's always preferred cooler weather with all that thick black fur. I'll need to find somewhere shady for us to rest before the heat builds much more. I reach the question mark and it looks as if someone's started to dismantle it, carefully though, stone by stone. We slump down in its shade and I take out my water bottle and sip, conscious of how little there is left. Still, I pour a little into my cupped palm and let Barney lap at it, his tongue gentle on my skin. Somewhere near here, there's a stone with a poem carved into it about the mist that so often weaved its way around these hills. There is no mist now, just the unrelenting sun.

I know I will die on this moor, sooner or later. I hope it's later. One day I will lie down on the heather and bracken and sink slowly down into the rich black peat below. The moor will cradle me beneath the crying curlews, little bits of heather tangling themselves in my hair. It will dye my fading hair darker again, as if the years have been wiped away, tan my pale skin for the first time. Fronds of bracken will wrap around my fingers, brush against my toes. Maybe my bones will slowly leach away, but the rest of me will be preserved, unlike everything that I wish I could have saved.

Contributors

Zay Alabi is a writer, musician and visual artist. They write stories that incorporate fantasy, sci-fi and horror elements into sprawling diverse worlds. The short story they wrote is based on the artwork of their fellow artist and dear friend Oliver Carter. In their dwindling free time they enjoy writing poetry about death, identity and impermanence while co-running literary events and workshops in Huddersfield. Their default state is diligently working on big ambitious creative projects and they adore the works of HP Lovecraft, much to the confusion of the people around them

Joseph Blythe is a Yorkshire writer of prose and poetry. His short story 'Still Bleeding' was included in *Stand* magazine, while his poetry has featured in collections by Grist Books and Livina Press. He is working on a pre-apocalyptic eco-novel as well as a fantasy novel, a poetry collection and various short stories. He hosts open mics at Grist Books' Literary Salons in Huddersfield and holds an undergraduate degree in English Literature with Creative Writing and a MA by Research in Creative Writing. He tweets and Instagrams @wooperark.

Ruth Cheesbrough grew up in Birmingham, just around the corner from a library, and spent a lot of her childhood reading. Her mother is from the west of Ireland and father was from Yorkshire and both places are important to her. She now lives in Bradford with her husband, teenage children, and several pets.

Gill Connors is a writer of poetry and prose. She has published two collections of poetry, *Tadaima* and *A Small Goodbye at Dawn*, both published by Yaffle. She is working on a new collection that will constitute part of her PhD on the subject of similarities between 16th century and 21st century women. She is currently writing a novel.

Michael Hargreaves writes short fiction and has featured in *The Other Stories* podcast, *The Nature of Cities* anthology and previous Grist anthologies. He has recently started a novel which he hopes to have finished by the end of 2024.

Matt Hill is an economic migrant to Bradford from London via Norfolk. After attending Michael Stewart's Invisible Writers Group in 2017 he collaborated on Leeds Lit Fest 2019's 'Tweeting a Tale for Found Fiction'. The same year he had his short story 'Losing Control' published in *Trouble: Grist Anthology of Protest*. 'Safety First' was his first published poem in Grist Books' *We're All In It Together: Poems for a DisUnited Kingdom* (2022).

Colin Hollis lives in Wakefield. Brought up in a Yorkshire coal mining village, he obtained a BSc in Physics at Sheffield University and worked in science labs, before a long career in teaching. He is a member of the writing group Black Horse Poets with Wakefield Word. He has two published novels and is presently completing a third. He takes a particular enjoyment in writing gentle short stories in the 2000-word range.

Ben Hramiak is an author with a Bachelor's Honours in English Literature and Creative Writing living and working in Yorkshire. He has written prose fiction from an early age and has been published in *Impspired* Volume 10, an anthology of short stories. He was also published in *New Contexts: 4*. He is currently working on a short novel set in feudal Japan. His writing style is best thought of as descriptive and succinct.

Gavin Jones is a writer and artist, living in Barnoldswick, which – depending on your opinion – is either in Yorkshire or Lancashire. Raised on the borders of Wales and England, he spent his formative years trudging the same streets as John Frost, Arthur Machen and Raymond Williams. He is currently writing the story of a cottage in the Yorkshire Dales and is a postgraduate researcher in Creative Writing at the University of Huddersfield.

Jack Leader was born in Blackpool in 2002 and is a burgeoning screenwriter currently pursuing studies in Screenwriting at the University of Huddersfield. As a student, Jack has actively contributed to both writing and directing various short films. Beyond the world of film, Jack has a penchant for writing short tales of horror and the occult. With an insatiable curiosity and love for the macabre, they look forward to continuing this theme with their screenplays.

M.E.G. (Matthew Ethan Gurteen) is a writer from the north of England. They are an English Literature researcher at the University of Huddersfield, focusing on murderers in the regional cultural memory. When not working on that, they can be found writing and editing their first horror novel. They have previously been published in several online poetry magazines and academic blogs. Follow them @megurteen for more.

Julie Noble's memoir piece 'Detail' was published in Kit de Waal's critically acclaimed *Common People* in 2019 and she won three awards, including a Northern Writers' Award. Her work has been published in *Mslexia*, *Writing Magazine* and internationally. In 2020, Claire Malcolm MBE recommended that Julie present 'My Name Is Julie' for BBC Radio 4 (still online). In 2021 she was selected for the GENESIS/JBW Emerging Writers Programme. Julie is currently writing plays, poems and prose.

Lydia Okell is a Chemistry student at the University of Huddersfield. They enjoy writing short stories in their spare time, and this is their first published work. Coming from the Isle of Man, Lydia has always been inspired by Manx folk tales to pursue the fantasy genre.

Mia Rayson Regan writes contemporary short stories and novels under a range of genres. Her writing often consists of difficult topics that she believes should be discussed. Mia has just completed an MA by Research in Creative Writing at the University of Huddersfield where she was awarded a scholarship. Her short story collection ties fairy tales to issues for young people in the modern day. Her poem 'The Cold Ring' was published with Grist Books in 2022. Mia's writers blog on Instagram is @words.of.a.writer

Dominic Rivron writes mainly short stories and poetry. He also writes reviews. His work has been published in a number of print and online magazines, including *The Beatnik Cowboy*, *International Times*, *The Milk House*, *Unlikely Stories* and *Stride Magazine*. He lives in the North of England.

Kate Squires is an emerging writer based in Yorkshire. She has written several short stories – often about the end of the world, and is currently working on her debut novel. Kate is happiest by the sea, and camping with her family and friends.

Ivor Tymchak grew up on a council estate, Ukraine inside the house and Yorkshire outside. His love of drawing gave him a ticket into the creative industries. He attended art school in Liverpool, Huddersfield, Portsmouth and Sheffield, graduating with a degree in film making. He became a musician, strip cartoon creator, graphic designer, caricaturist, stand-up comedian, compere, writer ... He still doesn't know what he wants to be when he grows up. He now lives in Wakefield.

William Thirsk-Gaskill is president of two writing groups in Wakefield. His Grist novella, *Escape Kit*, has been adapted and broadcast on BBC Radio 4. He is currently trying to find outlets for his second poetry collection, second short fiction collection, and his debut novel, which is about a pregnant android called Violet. He performs at as many open mic events as he can, and once in 2023 he was reimbursed for travelling expenses.

Michael Yates was environment reporter, then film critic at the *Sheffield Star*. He has had plays performed in Manchester, Liverpool, Sheffield, Leeds and at Wakefield Drama Festival. He was Writer in Residence when Bradford was UNESCO City of Film; and Poet in Residence in Mid-Yorkshire Hospitals in 2021, writing about COVID. He has published two books of short stories and three novels, including *Dying is the Last Thing You Ever Want to Do* in 2022.